TALES OUT OF

Birth of

by **David Leland**

Editor **Paul Kelley**
The Television Literacy Project

Contents

Cambridge University Press
Cambridge
London   New York   New Rochelle
Melbourne   Sydney

For Alan and Tom.
*In the hope that this nation will
stop beating its children.*

Introduction

Why study television?

Television and school occupy most of the waking life of
children. Television and school are the greatest influences on
children outside their immediate environment. Everyone
accepts the importance of school and considers it vital to
create an educational system that works. There has always
been debate about what should be taught, and how it should
be taught. On the other hand the position of television in the
lives of children never seems to raise the same questions:
how should television be organised for the education of
children? What should be shown? The debates about
children and television usually centre on 'sex and violence'
and whether children should be allowed to watch
programmes made for an adult audience. Contained within
this notion is the assumption that what adults want to see on
television will automatically deprave and corrupt children.

We are moving towards a world where both school and
television will be available to all children. The revolution that
this entails is far greater than the invention and spread of
printing, and far more rapid. Unlike reading, watching
television has an immediate and simultaneous impact – like
many people reading the same book at the same speed, and
at the same time. But to watch television there is no apparent
need to learn a complex code (as there is with language in
print), the images appear to speak for themselves and are
available to everyone. Four hundred years after the arrival of
the printing press we have only just reached the point where
more than half of the adults in the world can read. But in just
over fifty years more than half the world watches television.

Despite its popularity television has come in for some severe criticism. The printing press suffered a similar fate. It was said that printing would bring too many seditious and corrupting messages to the people, that it would destroy oral traditions, or that the wealthy would monopolise this means of communication. And there is more than a ring of truth in all these statements.

Whether the messages of television are constructive and to the general good largely depends on the inherent values of our society, of what we think to be 'good' and 'bad'. As I have said, the two issues most often singled out as targets are sex and violence. So often people who criticise television link sex and violence together and call them 'bad'. There is very little logic in these assertions. Violence is a destructive force and it is understandable that it should be considered 'bad'; however, sex is a pleasurable activity (and essential for procreation) and is logically 'good'. Others who criticise television draw attention to the negative way that women and the old are presented; the emphasis on certain groups (the well off, the police) and not others; the political slant given to news and documentaries; the way television avoids tackling many important issues; and the beliefs and behaviour they see as being encouraged by television.

Behind all these worries is the idea that television has an enormous influence on the people that watch it. It has been argued that this influence is greatest on the young, and this would seem logical. The young are not careful viewers. A good television viewer is one who knows how programmes are made and understands that most of what she sees on television is nothing like the 'real world'. If the young need to learn to be good viewers, they need to be taught. And if television is an influence on the young, shouldn't the television companies bear this in mind? Shouldn't they help the young become better viewers? And shouldn't they reconsider what is shown, what issues are raised on television?

Decisions about these questions are made by a small number of people, and in this television and education have much in common. They are both, either directly or indirectly,

3

instruments of political power, controlled by a tiny minority of people. Printing has been controlled in a similar way, but less so in recent years as the means of producing and reproducing the printed word have become more freely available.

People who control television are very preoccupied with the mass appeal of their programmes, by what might be called their product. Success is gauged by the product's ratings, how many people watched the programme. They cater for the mass audience, not individuals. Hence certain types of programmes that have proved popular – police series for example – are used over and over, and new types of programme are discouraged. The television companies often see their aim as selling a product, not helping viewers, and hence the idea of individuals with individual needs is lost. Many television commercials work by the paradox that one will only be individual if one joins the mass and buys a particular product. Success becomes linked to the product on offer. Schools function on a similar basis and, like television, they are not controlled by the consumers, the children – or even by their parents. They are determined by forces largely outside the individual's control.

The institutions of television, like the institutions of school and publishing, are all aimed at the many, and controlled by the few. They are institutions with their own social and political structures, and changes within such institutions are not easily achieved. These institutions do not change simply because they ought to change: and this is precisely the problem with television in schools.

Television and schools: why television isn't studied

Schools are the way they are for a number of different reasons. One is the pattern established hundreds of years ago in grammar schools of teaching academic subjects only – which didn't work then, and doesn't work now. Other constraints on schools are money, buildings, the choice of teachers and so on. If anyone wishes to change either how or what is taught in school they will face opposition. This opposition comes partly from those who resist change, who think that things are better as they are. These people tend to blame the child before they blame the system. Then there are those who have a vested interest in resisting change, from politically motivated organisations to the individual who believes that by protecting the system one is protecting one's job. Changes in what is taught in school (the curriculum) are not merely questions of teachers deciding that pupils ought to be taught something different, but of money and jobs. If a teacher has been appointed to a school to teach Latin, and given a budget and timetables to teach the subject, it is unlikely that they will want to cancel Latin in favour of Media Studies – or any other subject. Equally, changes in how subjects are taught are not easy to implement. Suppose it was found that languages are learnt more easily if the pupils learn in blocks of a month in which they do nothing but speak and read the language. Even if this were so, teachers taking other subjects that were easier to teach in small doses each day would hardly be keen to cancel their lessons. Questions of priority arise. Interdepartmental warfare is threatened. More important than these factors is the control that bigger educational institutions exert over education. In the UK this means examination boards, county councils, and the government. The government controls education directly through the Department of Education and Science, and indirectly in a range of different ways. For both political and bureaucratic reasons, none of these powerful institutions is keen on change. So it is not easy to change things in school, and although change does occur, it is usually a slow and painful process.

Looking at schools in terms of how they have responded to the changes in society in the last hundred years you might be forgiven for thinking that schools haven't changed at all. Except for a few, most schools appear not to take notice of such innovations as the invention and evolution of films, television, the automobile, technologies, and most of the social and industrial changes of the last century.

Televisions are used in schools and have become useful extensions of the teacher, with the added bonus of being able visually to transport the student to places and events outside the classroom. But the basic relationship between the student and the television has remained the same as that between the student and the teacher. The teacher and the television select the information and give it in predetermined forms to the student. But, as yet, there has been very little study in schools of television as a technological medium of expression and communication.

The problems facing the introduction of the study of television into schools as opposed to the introduction of schools programmes into schools are not made easier by the organisation of broadcasting. Television companies have not been created with education in mind – though there are one or two exceptions in the USA and Holland. Like other companies they are organised for profit and that means they are interested in attracting mass audiences. Even on news programmes the intent is often to attract the audience's attention – to keep them watching at any cost – rather than to educate or inform.

Television is also a tool of governments, a propaganda machine in the corner of every citizen's living-room. Programmes critical of government policy or which simply present an alternative point of view are often accused of bias and lack of balance. What constitutes balance, however, depends on where one draws the 'central' line within the spectrum of political opinion. What is 'central' in the UK is hardly 'central' in China. The point of balance is not a fixed point, but something that is manipulated and shifted. The politician who argues for balance is usually tampering with the scales. Governments are not keen to change television companies if it might run counter to their interests.

And what of changes in television companies themselves? Like schools, any attempt to change the priorities of television companies can also mean that jobs and money go from one part of the company to another, and that means people will resist change. So if people are trying to suggest that companies change their policy they may find that they get nowhere, and this is true of television for the young.

There are, of course, two kinds of television aimed at children: 'children's programmes', and 'schools programmes'. 'Children's programmes' tend to be imitations of adult programmes: drama, news, games shows and so on, all intended to capture a large audience. 'Schools programmes' are usually made for teachers, to help teach a curriculum that has nothing to do with teaching television. Curiously, in most of the world, it is illegal to use any television except school television in schools. And the reason that television programmes are not freed from copyright restrictions for use in schools is financial, not educational. The television companies do not want to pay further fees to those who made these programmes in order to remove the copyright restrictions.

The introduction of television/media studies into schools is a slow process: schools and television companies are not easy to change; the laws of copyright make the use of most television in schools illegal; and neither schools nor television are responsive to the needs of their consumers.

Television study, media studies

Despite these problems many teachers have tried to teach television in schools. These teachers argue that television and the media in general have a tremendous influence on children, and that children should be taught how to 'read' the media, and to understand the nature of the institutions that create the media. These teachers have faced tremendous problems. The use of television, pop music, radio, and photocopies of newspaper articles is illegal. Many other teachers see the media, and television in particular, as contrary to all the aims of education.

A curious prejudice exists amongst school teachers and the public at large that condemns the medium of communication, television, rather than the content or the structure of the television industry. There is nothing inherently wrong with television any more than printing or writing. When people have complaints against television what they usually mean is that they have complaints about particular programmes, or the people who control television. Of course, there are things wrong with television as there are with the ways in which television is manipulated and controlled. But it would be folly to conclude from this that the medium itself is inherently wrong.

Another problem facing those wishing to teach television is the nature of making television. It hs been shown that children understand television better if they make television or video programmes themselves – just as children learn to read and write at the same time. Children who have taken courses based on practical television work quickly learn what they see on television is no more than what the people who make programmes want them to see. They also quickly learn the limitations of the equipment itself. Television is only suitable for showing certain kinds of things. The equipment needed to do this is relatively expensive; its use is time-consuming, and involves children working co-operatively. All these factors conspire against practical television work being introduced into schools. Schools resist the introduction of courses that require a lot of money for obvious reasons. Work that requires more than the forty minutes to an hour usually allocated to a subject on the timetable creates problems that most schools don't want to deal with. Schools are organised around books and paper, including the time periods, and television work does not fit into this pattern. Finally, television, like film, is cooperative. This is a good thing, but for schools it poses difficulties because most schools are organised around the assessment of the individual's performance against a general yardstick. How do you measure the achievement of the individual when she is working in a group? Thus despite the clear evidence that to teach television properly you need to let children make their own television, practical work of this sort is very rare.

So not only do the teachers of media face the normal

resistance to change within school, they also face the added problems of the law, prejudice, and a subject that doesn't fit in easily with established school patterns. In order to overcome these limitations, teachers have tried to use existing systems. In the UK, teachers have established examination courses in the Media in order to gain respectability for the new subject. In the USA, teachers have argued that children need protection from television, and therefore it must be taught in schools. Nevertheless, given the unquestioned importance of television to children, very little has been done.

Tales out of School

Tales out of School are four films first broadcast on ITV: *Birth of a Nation*, *Flying into the Wind*, *Rhino* and *Made in Britain*. On the surface the release of this series seems to mark a new advance in the study of television. Now both the text and legal video of a major broadcast television production are available for use in schools. Already *Flying into the Wind* has been set for O level English Literature, and will be taught to thousands. And there can be no doubt that if this is followed by other broadcast material being released, it will be much easier to teach television in schools.

Obviously it is not as simple as this. Teaching the media, teaching television, is not just a matter of being able to discuss broadcast television. It needs to be part of an education system which is relevant to the society in which the children live. The introduction of broadcast television into schools will not achieve this. Television will only achieve its true significance when it is used as a practical means of expression and communication.

Take an example. *Birth of a Nation* is about school, and students know as much about school as anyone, if not more. So a logical question might be: is *Birth of a Nation* realistic? Is it 'true to life'? To answer this question a student might compare her experience in schools with the school shown in the film. Or someone might know that the events shown are, in fact, events that did happen in schools. In either case there is a hidden assumption that television is, or should be, realistic or 'true to life'.

Yet television is, obviously, not realistic or 'true to life'. Like other forms of literature it condenses and changes in order to make a certain kind of impact. Practical television work would make this clear. If one films an ordinary classroom on an ordinary day it would most probably be boring – nothing would happen. In television, as in literature in general, selection is a key process. There are also technical limitations to television equipment, and a film of an ordinary lesson may have very poor sound because the background noises of working – or not working. If students made their own film on school they would need to select material, arrange their filming so that the final product could be heard and seen, and most importantly, express a point of view about what they think school is – or should be. And this is exactly what *Birth of a Nation* does.

Television is both a creative and a practical process which can only be learned by trial and error. But many people feel that television is too complicated for the non-professional.

Most of us are passive receivers of whatever appears on our television screens. How the image gets there in the first place is something of a mystery. It is a complicated process which is carried out by 'professionals'. They are on the inside of the process, we are on the outside. Bearing in mind that most professionals are not beyond surrounding their work with a degree of mystique – mystique being an excellent form of protectionism – they are not necessarily the best people to turn to for instruction and guidance.

Of course, there is a vast amount of skill and expertise at work in television, but one does not have to be a professional to become actively involved in the process of making television and using it as a medium of communication.

It would be a considerable mistake to presume that to make television one must first acquire the skills and knowledge of the professional. Lightweight video cameras are now available of such superb quality and technical simplicity that they can be operated by a five year old with the minimum of interference from an adult. A three-hour tape can be put through the camera, recorded, played back, wiped and used again. Mistakes cost nothing.

Each time I watch young people using video cameras I see them breaking conventions and innovating new styles and techniques. There are very few rules in practical television: conventions, yes – rules, no. To pass on rules to be learned and followed would be like a blind man passing on his white stick to a person with eyes to see. Experts should be used as one uses a library, as a body of information to be referred to according to need. There is only one way to learn about television, and that is by doing it.

If *Tales out of School* become part of the curriculum, to be taught in the same way as part of the same system the four films attack, it will be both ironic and tragic. The films were released for use in schools in order to bring them to a wider audience, and to help children and teachers have freer access to television. Hopefully these four films will be used to help children discuss, criticise, and challenge the education they receive, the television they watch, and the television they make for themselves.

Paul Kelley
December 1985

Birth of a Nation was first transmitted on ITV in Britain on 19 June 1983. Given below are the credits and cast for this Central Independent Television production.

Credits

Production Manager	Donald Toms
1st Assistant Director	Guy Travers
Location Manager	Joanna Gollins
2nd Assistant Director	Roy Stevens
3rd Assistant Director	Chris Thompson
Production Assistant	Monica Rogers
Continuity	Melinda Rees
Camera Operator	Mike Miller
Camera Assistants	Alan Annand, Sue Gibson
Boom Operator	Tony Bell
Sound Assistant	Clive Osborne
Grip	Peter Hall
Dubbing Editor	Kevin Brazier
Costume Designer	Barbara Lane
Wardrobe	Daryl Bristow, Brian Cox
Assistant Art Director	Celia Barnett
Make-up Artist	Robin Grantham
Prop Buyer	Dawn Marsden
Property Master	Philip McDonald
Accountant	Joan Murphy
Sound Mixer	Tony Jackson
Dubbing Mixer	Mike Billing
Music by	Andy J. Clark
Production Executive	Sue Wall
Casting Director	Sheila Trezise
Editor	Steve Singleton
Art Director	Jamie Leonard
Photographed by	Ian Wilson
Associate Producer	Patrick Cassavetti
Written by	David Leland
Producer	Margaret Matheson
Directed by	Mike Newell

Geoff Figg	Jim Broadbent
Vic Griffiths	Robert Stephens
Twentyman	Bruce Myers
Mr Griff	Richard Butler
Mr Hodgeson	Fred Pearson
Miss Martlett	Peggyann Clifford
Mr James	William Hoyland
Barratt	Bruce Payne
Miss Denton	Kay Stonham
Whittaker	Ray Mort
Sgt Powell	Terry John
Miss Pointer	Gillian Davey
Alison Cooper	Suzanna Hamilton
Barry	Jesse Birdsall
Paul	Ian Roberts
Dawn	Juanita Waterman-Hutchinson
Terry	Michael Smart
George No 1	Robert Stagg
George No 2	Paul Gamble
Deputy Headmistress/	
Grunsell	Julia Deakin
Mr Kitchen	Michael Ames
Mr Grant	Peter Badger
Mrs Twentyman	Darryl Webster
Sylve	Lisa Geoghan
Stephen Harris	Tony Seaborne
Julie	Janet Lacey
Booth	Dean Macaree
Ramkissoon	Feizal Sobratty
Peter Field	Stuart Hunter
Martin Mills	Vincent Dawes
Sally Wilson	Julia Millbank
Cooper	Donald Dempster
King	Glenn Dallas
Alan Fraser	Danny Behrman
John	Errol Francis
Armitage	Jason Hood
Scott	Benjamin Perry
Ingram	Ian Searle
Margaret	Nicola Elliott

Birth of a Nation

Part One

1	**Exterior. Garden. Day.**	1

CHILDREN absorbed in play.

2	**Exterior. School gates. Day.**	2

St John's Comprehensive School on the outskirts of London.

Hundreds of CHILDREN streaming in one direction through the school gates towards the school.

Noise: voices, feet, traffic, a bell.

3	**Interior. School corridor. Day.**	3

A crush of CHILDREN make their way along the corridor: a certain amount of jostling, a lot of noise.

Directional arrows painted on the floor are totally ignored.

4	**Interior. Assembly hall. Day.**	4

A large assembly of PEOPLE: restless, and still a high quota of noise.
DEPUTY HEADMISTRESS GRUNSELL is at the front of the platform. Her job is to get total silence before the headmaster speaks.

GRUNSELL

Could we have some silence please? Now, whatever it is you have to say, I don't care how important it is, could we please try to behave like human beings. Quiet!

5 Int. The deputy headmaster's room. Day. 5

VIC GRIFFITHS is a large, overweight, shambling man with thick black, shaggy hair. He wears a rather old, dark suit; his shirt tends to part company with his loose fitting trousers, evidence of even fatter days.

His room is never tidy. He has a constant stream of visitors; there are mugs and a kettle for making coffee.

Along one wall there is a rough chart for next year's timetable. It is a vast, complex maze. VIC spends most of his time in the room staring and tampering with the chart.

VIC is staring at the chart. Smoking a Gold Flake. Deep concentration on order.

6 Ext. School gates. Day. 6

JANE and TOM TWENTYMAN drive up to the school gates in their Ford Fiesta.

TOM TWENTYMAN is a school teacher: a somewhat introvert person, forty years old, soberly dressed.

They get out of the Fiesta. From the back of the car, TWENTYMAN takes first his briefcase, and then a glass case containing a large, stuffed cormorant.

JANE takes over the driving position in the car. She is in the advanced stages of pregnancy. JANE drives off in the car. TWENTYMAN walks towards the school.

MR GRIFF, the head, addresses the school.

Posted along each side of the hall are various MEMBERS OF STAFF. Their job is to keep order and to single out trouble makers.

During the HEADMASTER's address a couple of TEACHERS on patrol pick their way along the rows of PUPILS, touch a couple of them on the shoulder, and remove them from the main group to stand conspicuously beside them at the end of the row.

> GRIFF
> I would remind you all that this term is an exam term – CSEs, O levels, A levels – the most important time in the school calendar. A time when people's future careers will be decided. This is why you are here –

GRIFFITHS is concentrating on his chart, and smoking another Gold Flake.

A BOY comes into the room. GRIFFITHS takes this in, but does not break his concentration.

> GRIFFITHS
> What do you want, Barry?

> BARRY
> Mr Meighan sent me, sir.

> GRIFFITHS
> What for?

> BARRY
> Spitting on someone in the playground, sir, but it was an accident.

GRIFFITHS
(cutting his concentration on the chart and
moving towards the door)
We should be in assembly.

| 9 | **Int. Assembly hall. Day.** | 9 |

GRIFF
In many ways, this school is like the nation. There
are far too many people who are content to get
away with seven out of ten. With more attention,
more concentration, with harder work, these
people could easily get eight out of ten. And
higher. Not that I will be thanked for pointing that
out to them, or for pushing them forwards when
the going gets tough. No. I calculate that the
difference between being a great nation and being
a mediocre nation lies somewhere between nine
and seven out of ten.

| 10 | **Int. Corridor. Day.** | 10 |

GRIFFITHS and BARRY make their way along the empty
corridors towards the assembly hall.

They pass ELIZABETH MARTLETT, Mr Griff's personal
assistant, who is making her way towards the assembly hall.
ELIZABETH is very large and not noted for moving at high
speeds.

GRIFFITHS
Good morning, Miss Martlett.

MARTLETT
Good morning, Mr Griffiths.

As they turn the corner, STEPHEN HARRIS (14) dodges out
from a doorway and cuts into the boys' lavatory.

HARRIS is alone. He lights a cigarette. He is a dark haired, sallow youth with a moustache.

He is impressed by the pristine condition of the toilet.

>   HARRIS
> Very . . . very . . . nice.

He takes out a magic marker and writes 'NICE' on the white wall.

>   HARRIS
> N . . . I . . . C . . . E.

He goes into a cubicle. He is surprised to find there is a lock on the door.

>   HARRIS
>   (locking the door)
> Great.

He sits on the toilet seat and opens a pocket version of *Playbirds*.

POLICE SERGEANT POWELL of the local force, is addressing the school.

>   POWELL
> I know I am addressing only a small minority
> among you but what I want to say to that minority
> is: stop. Think. What I want to say to *all* of you is
> how glad I am to be here with you this morning.
> The British system of policing relies heavily on
> your cooperation and approval. When you leave
> this school, you will all become citizens in our
> society, and as citizens you will all have an active
> role to play.

GRIFFITHS joins GEOFF FIGG (35), an English teacher, who is posted at the back of the hall near one of the exit doors.

> GRIFFITHS
> What's this then?

> FIGG
> Local bank manager.

> GRIFFITHS
> What's he doing?

> FIGG
> He's offering them interest free bank loans the first three years after they leave school – pay it back out of their dole money.

> POWELL
> (during the above)
> Every citizen has the freedom to do and say anything. But this does not mean you are free to say and do what you like, when you like, where you like. There is no such thing as complete freedom. You are free to say and do as you please *so long as it is within the law*.

At the back:

> GRIFFITHS
> What's brought all this on?

> FIGG
> Eighth commandment – thou shalt not nick from the local Paki sweetshop.

> GRIFFITHS
> Eh.

> FIGG
> What?

> GRIFFITHS
> (leans over)
> The Incredible Bulk . . . behind you.

19

FIGG looks over his shoulder to see ELIZABETH MARTLETT's face pressed against the glass window in the door. The two men turn their attention to POLICE SERGEANT POWELL.

> POWELL
> (during the above)
> The laws of our country are not designed to oppress but to safeguard your freedoms. The function of the police is to enforce the law. Any reduction in the ability of the police to enforce the law results in reduction in the freedom of every member of society.

> POWELL
> (after the above)
> As citizens, you have duties as well as rights. It is the citizen's duty to obey the law, to keep the peace and to assist the police who act for the good of society as a whole. If a person sees a crime being committed or –

There is a scream and general panic from the centre of the hall followed by a bang. Somebody has ignited a firework. General chaos. TEACHERS dive in to find the culprits.

13   Int. Boys' lavatory. Day.   13

After assembly: the toilet is crowded, a lot of noise.

MARTIN MILLS, a small 12-year-old, is taking a wee. STEPHEN HARRIS comes out of the cubicle and occupies the stall next to MILLS.

Two pee holes down from MILLS, JOHN INGRAM (14) is also taking a wee. He does not hear the conversation between MILLS and HARRIS.

> HARRIS
> Oi. You bring me 10p by tomorrow or I'll cut your cock off . . .

MILLS looks up at HARRIS, then at HARRIS's cock and then down again at his own.

In the background, a youth (BOOTH) is banging on one of the toilet doors.

> BOOTH
> Open up Feisal, I want a shit.

> RAMKISSOON
> Bugger off.

> HARRIS
> . . . with my penknife.

BOOTH walks up and down banging on the toilet doors.

> MILLS
> I gave you 10p before half term.

> HARRIS
> And you still got your cock so what you
> complaining about?

HARRIS leaves the lavatory.

> BOOTH
> Come on, Feisal, you nurd, you been in there
> bloody hours.

At the same time: INGRAM leaves the lavatory. As he walks past MILLS, who is still trying to squeeze out a wee, INGRAM trips MILLS so that he sprawls into the stall. Also, BOOTH takes a flying kick at one of the lavatory doors.

> RAMKISSOON
> Bloody hell!

As HARRIS goes out of the door, BARRATT (the PE master) picks up on the noise and barges his way into the toilet. INGRAM stands politely to one side, then slips out into the corridor.

> BARRATT
> Right. Hold it! Booth! Mills!

FIGG walks along the corridor; he is looking for his class. He always carries a plastic carrier bag full of books and so on.

He stops outside a particular classroom where a 12-year-old BOY is standing outside the door in the corridor. FIGG looks into the classroom through the window in the upper part of the door.

> FIGG
> (to the BOY)
> What are you?

> BOY
> Cheeky, sir, and stupid.

> FIGG
> No, what class are you?

> BOY
> B1, sir.

> FIGG
> What are you doing here?

> BOY
> Chucked out.

> FIGG
> For being cheeky?

> BOY
> And stupid, sir.

> FIGG
> I see.

FIGG walks off.

FIGG proceeds down another long corridor, passing a

14-year-old BOY standing outside a classroom.

His attention is drawn by something in the centre of the corridor which he stops to inspect.

>   BOY
>   (from the other end of the corridor)
>   Turds, sir.

>   FIGG
>   I do believe you're right, brother.

>   BOY
>   Goat's turds.

16   Int. Classroom. Day.   16

MR JAMES (40) is a Maths teacher and he is working with an O-level group of 14–15-year-olds who are about to sit their exams. He is a strong authoritarian figure who commands respect. He is writing numbers on the blackboard, explaining how to convert to base 5.

JAMES's attention is drawn towards the door where he sees FIGG looking into the classroom. FIGG half nods and moves on.

17   Int. Corridor. Day.   17

FIGG looks into another classroom. This is TWENTYMAN's Rural Studies room.

A first-year GROUP is involved in various activities in different parts of the room.

In the centre of the room, surrounded by several CHILDREN, is the GOAT responsible for the turds in the corridor. Pick up on MILLS.

Somewhere, among all the activity, is TWENTYMAN.

The lesson is still in progress. Close shot of MR JAMES.

Attention in the class is far from perfect. There is a certain amount of muted chat among the PUPILS and the attention of two of the GIRLS is drawn to the view of the main gate from the window. INGRAM is concentrating hard upon the lesson.

MR JAMES is not a person to suffer noise and disruption easily. He stops writing on the blackboard. He puts down the chalk, picks up the board rubber and wipes off his work. He walks to the window and looks out and down towards the gate. This abrupt change of action takes the attention of most of the class. There is a concealed threat in the entire manoeuvre.

> JAMES
> I want you all to come to this side of the class and look out of the window. Quietly! Whatever is done in this class will be done quietly . . .

Everybody has stopped in mid-action.

> JAMES
> Right.

They move to the window. When everybody is in position:

> JAMES
> Down there, at the gate – if you cannot see, Margaret, come and stand here.

> MARGARET
> I'm alright down here, sir.

> JAMES
> Come and stand here, please. I don't want to argue with you about it.

MARGARET moves to stand near JAMES.

We get a view of the main gate as JAMES speaks.

> JAMES

Take a good look. Down there, hanging about for
no good reason, can be seen a colourful selection
of those among us who failed to acquire
qualifications before setting foot in the real world.
As you can see –

> MARGARET

John McCarthy got CSEs.

> JAMES

Margaret – a CSE is to an O level what lard is to
butter – these people are reduced to hanging
around at the school gate looking back on lost
opportunities. Sit down. Quietly.

THE CLASS go to their seats. JAMES has not finished. They
sense danger, they know when JAMES is angry.

> JAMES

I have no time for failures. Noise and disorder are
the enemies of learning. There is going to be order
in this classroom and there is going to be
discipline because this class is going to leave the
protection of this school with a requisite minimum
number of O levels beneath its belt. The choice is
work – or the rabble. Any person anxious to join
the rabble may do so now.
>> (slight pause)
We have wasted time.

JAMES returns to his work at the blackboard.

We focus on the gathering of YOUNG PEOPLE at the gate.

A classroom full of PUPILS (14–15), no teacher in attendance, noisy.

Everybody is sitting around and chatting; there is quite a large group over by the window. Two GIRLS are leaning out of the window and shouting to the GROUP at the gate. Two or three BOYS are busy drumming on desk tops.

FIGG looks through the window in the door and then comes into the classroom. He has to shout above the noise.

Although characters are given lines, their words are part of the general talk and noise evident throughout the scene.

Pick up on STEPHEN HARRIS who tends to sit back and say nothing.

> FIGG
> What are you?

> JULIE
> What?

> FIGG
> What class are you?

> JULIE
> Eh?

> FIGG
> (loud)
> Can you shut it for a sec? Great. Thanks.

It is still far from quiet.

> FIGG
> Are you A4?

> JULIE
> (with others)
> Yeah.

> FIGG
> What are you doing in here, you're supposed to be
> on the fourth floor?

General response, everybody telling roughly the same story,
all speaking and shouting at the same time. They explain that
they were on the fourth floor. They were moved by Mrs
Denton who said they shouldn't have been in that classroom
so they were made to stand around in the corridor where
they were told off for making a noise. They were then sent
down to this floor after someone had been to see the
Incredible Bulk (Elizabeth Martlett). They are all innocent.
Nothing can be blamed onto them. It is not their fault.

> FIGG
> OK, so we'll stay in here. My name's –

> BOY
> Why were you late, sir?

> FIGG
> Well, as you know, there was a terrorist attack in
> assembly, and we've been sorting out the bits of
> arms and legs, and I lost my timetable and had to
> get one from the office which is like trying to get
> an interview with the Pope . . . Right, my name is
> Geoff Figg and I know all the gags about figs, most
> of them filthy and I'll tell you them all another
> day. I've not taught you lot before, I've only been
> here a term and a half – are you going to sit at your
> places or does everyone want to sit on the window
> sill?

He moves HARRIS and a couple of the others from the
window sill. BOOTH, the youth responsible for damaging the
lavatory door, comes into the classroom.

> FIGG
> Hello, where have you been?

> BOOTH
> To see Vic.

FIGG

Right. Sit down. OK, any of you taking O levels?

Derision and laughter.

FIGG

Right. Is there anyone here taking CSEs?

A few hands go up. COOPER, the classroom clown, is heading for the door.

FIGG

Where are you going?

COOPER

To do a wee wee, sir.

Some laughter, COOPER is encouraged.

FIGG

Have you got your matches and are you coming back?

COOPER

I don't need matches to do a wee wee, sir.

FIGG

Let's not get into it now – what's your name?

COOPER

Wee Wee, sir.

Laughter.

FIGG

Right, you'd better go and do your wee wee. Wee Wee.

Some PUPILS pick up on this and start to call Cooper 'Wee Wee'. COOPER grins but begins to feel as if he might have made a mistake. He passes RAMKISSOON who is on his way into the classroom.

FIGG

Where have you been?

RAMKISSOON
To see Vic.

FIGG
Right. What's your name?

RAMKISSOON
Ramkissoon, sir.

BOOTH
No, it's Feisal, sir.

RAMKISSOON
(gives him a shove)
Shut up.

FIGG
(to the class)
OK, what were you working on last term, before
half term that is?

General uncertainty, no answers.

FIGG
Who was teaching you last term?

Among other replies:

SYLVE
Mr Bartholomew.

RAMKISSOON
No, it wasn't.

SYLVE
It was Mr Bartholomew, clever sod. We had Mr
Bartholomew and then Mr Wier and he was
swopped over with – what was her name?

JULIE
I dunno, do I?

RAMKISSOON
Miss Dunn.

SYLVE
Miss Dunn.

BOOTH
She been dun.

SYLVE
(to Booth)
Clever sod.

FIGG
So you had different teachers.

SYLVE
What did I just say?

FIGG
What did you do with these teachers?

PUPILS
Nothing/Read a book/Chucked them out/Piss all.

SYLVE
Oi! Bleedin swearing.

FIGG
You read books.

RAMKISSOON
No, the teacher read books.

FIGG
What did you do?

RAMKISSOON
Copying out.

SYLVE
That's what we do, we do copying out.

FIGG
What?

SYLVE
I dunno.

> FIGG
> Do you have a text book? What do you copy out?

> BOOTH
> A book.

> FIGG
> What book, what is it called?

Pause. General uncertainty.

> RAMKISSOON
> *Hard Times*.

> FIGG
> You're joking. *Hard Times?*

General agreement about the title.

> FIGG
> Who's that by?

No response.

> FIGG
> Who wrote it?

> SYLVE
> Don't you know?

> FIGG
> I was asking the class, as a general question, do you know who wrote *Hard Times*?

> SYLVE
> You're the bloody teacher, you ought to know. I just copied it out.

> FIGG
> Does anybody here know who wrote *Hard Times*?

Slight pause. Nobody has the answer.

Empty corridor.

The bell rings.

B GROUP stampede down the corridor. C GROUP (first years) hurl themselves out of Twentyman's classroom and join the rush.

HODGESON is walking along the corridor in the opposite direction. He grabs a couple of BOYS, shakes them, and shouts at all of them in a very loud voice.

> HODGESON
> Walk! You walk along the corridors – do you hear? Everybody walk!

THE BOYS stop running but continue at speed down the corridor with a heel-toe fast walk. As soon as they turn the corner they break into a run.

HODGESON stands at the door of Twentyman's classroom. The GIRLS leave the classroom at a leisurely pace. Some of the girls are clearing up.

Although his attention is caught by various attractions, including the GOAT, HODGESON does not like Twentyman's classroom. He distrusts it.

> HODGESON
> I thought you were in the lab.

> TWENTYMAN
> It turned out better to be in here.

> HODGESON
> This is your Rural Studies room.

> TWENTYMAN
> Yes.

HODGESON
When taking a Science class I think it better to be in the Science laboratory, less confusing all round. We have discussed it before.

TWENTYMAN
Yes.

HODGESON
Do you have a free period now?

TWENTYMAN
Yes.

HODGESON
I'd like a talk in, say, five minutes.

TWENTYMAN
Where – here?

HODGESON
Staffroom – it'll be quiet in there.

22   Int. Boys' changing room. Day.   22

First year BOYS are tearing off their clothes and getting into shorts and singlets. No fun, serious business.

Pick up on PETER FIELD, moving fast trying to stay with the rest.

A lot of noise, some pushing, argument. As soon as a boy is changed he makes for the changing room door.

FIELD takes 11p (5p + 3 × 2p) from his pocket, holds it in his hand, and makes for the doorway.

Throughout the following sequence we pick up on FIELD, watch his reactions; he stays in the middle of the pack for protection, he watches other children's reactions, joins in when it is necessary.

First year GIRLS are taking Domestic Science with MISS
POINTER.

> POINTER
> (writing on the blackboard)
> Royal pudding. You can all write this down. 225
> grams of flour, 175 grams of suet – chopped fine –
> four eggs . . .

24   Int. Gymnasium. Day.   24

Aerial view: the first BOY runs into the gymnasium followed
by other BOYS: they sit cross-legged in the centre of the
gymnasium floor.

As the group builds, the PE master, BARRATT, dressed in
track suit and trainers, steps into view.

The last BOY comes in through the doorway. This is SCOTT
who is not very good at gymnastics due to poor coordination.

A roar goes up from the group as SCOTT comes in through
the door.

> BARRATT
> Last in, Scott.

> SCOTT
> No, sir.

> BARRATT
> Yes, sir. Don't argue Scott, yes, sir.

SCOTT runs away from BARRATT. They circle the group.

> SCOTT
> No, sir.

> BARRATT
> Come here, Scott.

> SCOTT
> I'm not, sir, no . . .

BARRATT makes for the boy. A roar goes up from the group.BARRATT chases SCOTT round the gym and hits him on the head with the class register. A cheer. He catches him, makes him bend over, then kicks his behind. A bigger cheer. During this, the genuine LAST ARRIVER slips into the class.

SCOTT sits down to the cheers and boos of the group. BARRATT blows his whistle.

25   Int. Staffroom. Day.   25

HODGESON and TWENTYMAN are sitting in the staffroom. The room is quiet, most of the teachers are in class.

In the background MR JAMES is meticulously marking exercise books. He smokes a cigarette which he does not remove from his mouth.

> HODGESON
> I've been looking through C1's books, Tom, and you've not been marking them.

> TWENTYMAN
> I have . . . marked the books.

> HODGESON
> Well, let's take a look, shall we? Here – at random – this is very shoddy work – this is John Langley, is it?

> TWENTYMAN
> Yes, he's a bright boy.

> HODGESON
> It would help me if you put these in alphabetical order. You say he's bright but his book's a mess. I can hardly read his name and there's graffiti on the cover.

TWENTYMAN
Isn't it more important he gets down what he's
trying to say?

HODGESON
No. The first priority is that he understands the
rudiments of the curriculum. If he's simply writing
down what you've written on the blackboard, he's
not trying to *say* anything, is he? There's no excuse
for shoddy work, but let's not get side tracked.
The point is there are no marks in his book.

TWENTYMAN
Yes, there are marks.

HODGESON
Show me.

TWENTYMAN
Here, 'good work'. Another there, 'I've got a book
on this – ask me'.

HODGESON
Those are not marks, Tom.

TWENTYMAN
You mean grades.

HODGESON
Yes, sorry, I'll say that again. You have not been
grading the books, have you?

TWENTYMAN
No, I have not been grading the books, but I have
been marking them.

HODGESON
From now on, please grade their work.

TWENTYMAN
You want me to rank them, put them into order?

HODGESON
Yes. And I want you to test them. This week. I've prepared the questions, no further preparation is required.

TWENTYMAN
(getting up)
I only took on Science as a second subject, to help out the department. I teach Rural Studies, that's my subject.

HODGESON
I've not finished yet, Tom. We have to pick over the sticky subject of sex.

26   Int. Gymnasium. Day.   26

The first year GROUP is running round in a circle in the centre of the gymnasium. BARRATT is at the periphery, a whistle in the corner of his mouth. He holds an old plimsoll, size 12. BARRATT blasts on the whistle.

BARRATT
Faster! Come on, faster! Faster!

There now follows a mad, violent dash around the gymnasium. The BOYS are required to touch the centre of the four walls of the gymnasium and then to rush back and to sit cross-legged in the centre of the floor. The last one to sit down gets a belt with the slipper.

27   Int. Domestic Science room. Day.   27

Close-up of mixing bowl full of flour and suet.

POINTER
Having made your hole, you put in your yolks.

She pours four egg yolks into the bowl.

The BOYS hurl themselves round the gymnasium. A mad, violent dash.

> BARRATT
> Come on!

BARRATT stands in the centre of the gym – he gets genuine pleasure from this game – he believes the boys enjoy it too.

BOYS throw themselves to the ground in a circle round BARRATT's feet. ARMITAGE is the last one home.

> BARRATT
> Armitage.

> ARMITAGE
> No . . .

A cheer of relief from the crowd. ARMITAGE, who is wearing a shirt instead of a singlet, is pulled out of the group by BARRATT and made to bend over. He is belted on the behind with the slipper.

> BARRATT
> Where's your singlet, Armitage?

> ARMITAGE
> Lost, sir.

> BARRATT
> Lost? Lost?! My class takes pride in its appearance, boy. Off! Get it off. Come on lad we haven't got all day.

ARMITAGE pulls off the shirt. He is rather thin. The rest of the class find this funny.

> BARRATT
> Quiet! No singlet. Over.

ARMITAGE braves it out and bends over. BARRATT hits him with the slipper and knocks him forwards. The CLASS laugh.

The recipe for Royal pudding is written up on the blackboard:

ROYAL PUDDING

225g of flour
175g of suet – chopped fine
3 tablespoons of Demerara sugar
4 eggs – separated
85g of apricot jam
85g of marmalade
57g of mixed dried fruit
Grated lemon rind
Nutmeg

Serves 10

The CLASS is watching the teacher make the Royal pudding.
There is a faint air of boredom.

> POINTER
> (mixing ingredients in a bowl)
> If you put it in too quickly it goes lumpy, you
> should know that. Yes – what's your name?

> SALLY
> Sally Wilson . . . miss.

> POINTER
> Yes, Sally, what is it?

> SALLY
> Why are we watching, miss?

> POINTER
> Watching what?

> SALLY
> Watching you make the pudding, miss. Last term
> we used to make things.

> POINTER
> Last term the school could afford to subsidise your

POINTER *(continued)*
parents to let you make things, Sally; this term it
can't. This term, you're lucky you can watch me
make things . . . and I'm lucky to be here to make
them.

30   Ext. The school gate. Day.   30

A long view of the school gate. Standing around, talking,
smoking, a GROUP of fifteen young people, male/female/black/
white.

This GROUP gradually grows.

It's quiet: traffic noises in the background, and then the
school bell.

31   Ext. Playground. Day.   31

Noise. A mass of YOUNG PEOPLE standing around, playing,
running, etc. A TEACHER on patrol floats through the shot.

In the distance, we focus on HARRIS and MILLS. We watch
the action as part of the overall playground activity.

                    HARRIS
When you see me coming you stand up, right?
Right?

                    MILLS
Yes.

                    HARRIS
And you do as you're told or I'll stick my pen knife
up your arse and I bloody mean it. And you call
me Baron – right? Call me Baron, now. Do it.

                    MILLS
Baron.

                    HARRIS
Say, 'yes, Baron'.

MILLS
Yes, Baron.

HARRIS
And you pay your subs, that's 10p anytime I ask for it, or I'll cut your stupid cock off.

HARRIS punches MILLS in the gut.

HARRIS
Got it?

32   Int. Science laboratory. Day.   32

TWENTYMAN teaching first year GROUP B1.

He is writing up a list on the blackboard.

TWENTYMAN
At the end of the week there is going to be a test. I am writing up a list of subjects upon which you will be tested together with the questions. If you wish to do well in the test, write down the list and the questions and prepare your answers. If anybody needs help, ask me or help each other.

33   Int. Vic's room. Day.   33

FIGG
There's this constant dribble – Booth, Feisal and Company, the cream of the 'A' stream, flowing in and out of my class down here to get their arses whacked.

GRIFFITHS
Then don't send them.

FIGG
I don't send them! It's not me. It's for crimes committed while in the act of studying wool yields in Australia . . . and maths. Why can't people keep their kids straight?

GRIFFITHS
It's all in the staff handbook. Tony Kitchen and me, the two Deputy Heads, are the official whackers, and no other people can lay a hand on the pupils' arses – it's all in the book.

FIGG
There's always a bigger queue outside your door.

GRIFFITHS
Griff's life's in there and I've lost it. Tony takes his work more seriously – he takes a run up before he lays it on.

FIGG
It's buggering up my classes, Vic.

A BOY is standing in the doorway.

GRIFFITHS
What do you want, John?

JOHN
Mr James sent me to you, sir.

GRIFFITHS
What for?

JOHN
Eating, sir.

FIGG
Eating?

GRIFFITHS
Eating in class, were you?

JOHN
Yes.

GRIFFITHS
What were you eating?

JOHN
Chewing gum and chocolate, sir.

GRIFFITHS
Together?

JOHN
Yes.

GRIFFITHS
Have you done this before, in class?

JOHN
Yes.

GRIFFITHS
And Mr James caught you and warned you before,
did he?

JOHN
Yes, and for talking. He told me to tell you I'm a
blabbermouth.

GRIFFITHS
A what?

JOHN
A blabbermouth.

GRIFFITHS
Well, you don't look like a blabbermouth to me,
John, but then who am I to contradict Mr James?
You're in the first year, aren't you?

JOHN
Yes.

GRIFFITHS
And you're twelve years old.

JOHN
Yes.

GRIFFITHS
And because you're twelve years old, John, I have
to say this to you, John – very grave this – because
you are a child of twelve tender years, I have to

GRIFFITHS *(continued)*
ask you this. Now, do you want me to get in touch
with your mother and father and tell them about
your being a blabbermouth, or would you rather
take the soft option and have a slap of the slipper?
It's up to you, John.

JOHN
Slipper please, sir.

GRIFFITHS
Right, I knew you'd see sense.
(getting up, brisk, takes out the slipper)
You're nothing if not polite, John. Now, bend over.

JOHN bends over. VIC smacks him lightly.

GRIFFITHS
Now off you go and tell Mr James I gave you one
slap of the slipper for being a blabbermouth, and
that I've put it in the punishment book.

JOHN
Thank you, sir.

JOHN leaves the office. VIC makes an entry into the
punishment book. The bell goes.

FIGG
Do you always lay it on like that?

GRIFFITHS
Little strokes for little arses.

FIGG
Why bother?

GRIFFITHS
It's quick and it's easy.

FIGG
So is gas.

They leave the office.

34   Int. Science laboratory. Day.   34

The room is empty except for TWENTYMAN. TWENTYMAN leaves the classroom, picking up his briefcase as he goes.

The blackboard has been wiped clean.

35   Ext. Playground. Day.   35

An open area which leads to a block which houses, among other classrooms, the Chemistry laboratory. FIGG and GRIFFITHS are walking to the block. This is a break between classes, there are no children at play.

> FIGG
> If other teachers can't keep their kids straight, not my problem, brother. I don't want them bending over in your office when they should be in my class. How do I stop it?

> GRIFFITHS
> You serious?

> FIGG
> Yeah.

> GRIFFITHS
> You'll not be popular.

> FIGG
> Come on, how do I fix it?

> GRIFFITHS
> Christ knows. Sounds like a memo job. You'll have to negotiate with the Bulk.

> FIGG
> Why her?

> GRIFFITHS
> She writes out the memos – and she's got the key to the photostat machine. In her knickers.

MARTLETT is at the typewriter. A young woman, ALISON
COOPER (18) taps on the glass of the service hatch.

As they speak, WHITAKER, who is the School Bursar, comes
out of the Headmaster's study. We glimpse GRIFF sitting in
his study.

> COOPER
> Is it convenient for me to see Mr Griff?

> MARTLETT
> What's it about?

> COOPER
> My name is Alison Cooper, I'm an ex-pupil.

> MARTLETT
> Oh, Alison, I remember, yes. Didn't recognise you
> for a moment. You've changed. Your hair's
> different.

> COOPER
> Yes.

> MARTLETT
> (to secretary)
> This is Alison Cooper. How are your parents?

> COOPER
> Very well, thank you. Is it possible for me to see
> Mr Griff?

> MARTLETT
> Today, I'm afraid not. I couldn't even squeeze you
> in. But I could put you in next week. Are you in a
> hurry?

> COOPER
> Any time will do.

> MARTLETT
> How about next Tuesday? Two-thirty. Right?

An O-level class is waiting outside the Chemistry laboratory.
They are in small groups on either side of the corridor.

HODGESON is late. He moves at speed down the corridor
towards the waiting PUPILS.

> HODGESON
> Who left this door open?

He spots several BOYS in the classroom; they are all trying to
read one book.

> HODGESON
> Out. All of you – out!

The BOYS go back into the corridor, except INGRAM, who
hides behind the door.

> HODGESON
> In a line, in a line. That is what the arrow means –
> you line up in a civilised and orderly manner,
> along here, *in a line*. Not sprawl around like thugs
> and prostitutes on a street corner.

HODGESON waits for silence and order.

> HODGESON
> Alright, in you go.

They file silently into the laboratory. INGRAM, hiding behind
the door, makes it to a seat without being detected by
HODGESON.

---

38   **Int. Classroom. Day.**   **38**

FIGG is writing a list up on the blackboard. A4 is walking into
the classroom, there is quite a lot of noise.

HODGESON makes his entrance into the Chemistry
laboratory.

>   HODGESON
> Good morning, 4C.

>   CLASS
> Good morning, Mr Hodgeson.

HODGESON walks to the desk. He sees the book which is
lying there.

>   HODGESON
> Where did this come from?

Silence.

>   HODGESON
> Ingram.

>   INGRAM
> I wasn't looking at it Mr Hodgeson.

ALISON COOPER looks into the lab through the class door
windows.

HODGESON puts the book into his briefcase. INGRAM sits
down, having escaped trouble once again.

40   Int. Classroom. Day.   **40**

FIGG goes through the list he has written up on the
blackboard. He has to fight for order, which may mean
breaking off and asking for quiet, etc.

FIGG's attention is periodically attracted to ALAN FRASER (14)
with blond hair, who has a rather intense concentrated look
on his face. (He is wanking.)

FIGG

Listen, we're not really supposed to be doing this, so if you scream or chuck bricks out of the window somebody's bound to come and sort us out, so a certain amount of hush will keep us all out of trouble. Right? Right.

(reads down the list)

CLASS – now that's not this type of class, though it may have something to do with it. It's the ruling class, the middle class, the working class, CLASS. Pay attention, Anna. POLITICS. SEXUAL EQUALITY. RACE RELATIONS – a black granny in Bradford. CHILDREN'S RIGHTS – have you got any? UNEMPLOYMENT. RIOTS – people in the streets killing each other – RIOTS. WAR. THE RED XHOSA.

BOOTH
(and others)

The what? Red what?

FIGG

The Red Xhosa. They're an African tribe.

BOOTH

King!

KING

Shut it, Booth.

FIGG

They have fighting rituals. They settle all their fights with sticks, all the young men carry sticks.

BOOTH

What you need a stick for when you can kick 'em in the bollocks?

ALISON COOPER looks in through the window.

SYLVE
Do you want us to copy that down, sir?

SEVERAL PEOPLE
Shut up, Sylve.

FIGG
Now, this is a list you can add to. This is a list of subjects we're going to discuss.

SYLVE
Yeah, but do you want us to copy it down?

FIGG
Plastic grass.

JULIE
Yeah, they've got that in the precinct down Percival Way.

FIGG
That's right.

SYLVE
We all know that.

JULIE
Dogs' mess all over it and it takes months to go away.

SYLVE
I've seen it.

JULIE
Just sits there stinking.

BOOTH
Cor, lay off!

FIGG
(to Sylve)
What do you think about plastic grass? Do you like it?

SYLVE
(feeling as if she's been accused of
something)
. . . I dunno. We ain't got a dog.

HARRIS
You're a dog, Sylve.

SYLVE
Shut up.
(to Figg)
Do you want us to copy that down or not?

HARRIS
Up your box, Sylve.

FIGG
No, Sylve, I don't want you to spend the lesson
copying out, I think we've got better things we can
do with our time – but you have a choice.
(to the class)
You can spend the lesson copying out or you can
spend it discussing these or any other subjects
which may interest you . . . alright, Sylve?

SYLVE
I don't care. I'm not here because I want to be
here. It ain't nothing to do with me. What you
starting on me for?

HARRIS
She's thick.

SYLVE
What do you know, clever bollocks?

HARRIS
Sod all.

> SYLVE
> If I'm thick, so are you. We're all thick, that's why
> we're in this class, 'cos we're thick, so up you.
> Don't ask me no questions. You're the teacher.
> You got to take it out of your head and put it into
> mine. That's your job. You're the teacher.

> KING
> Listen to it.

> SYLVE
> Coon.

> KING
> Bollocks.

> FIGG
> Right. The usual for an essay is two sides with a
> special of five. I expect a minimum of five sides
> and a special of fifteen.

Stunned reaction.

> FIGG
> But that's not today. That's not tomorrow or even
> this week. So forget about it. Today, sit back,
> relax, do nothing, just talk.

41   Ext. School playground. Day.   41

In the main playground looking down towards the main
gate.

ELIZABETH MARTLETT is staring down towards the gathering
of YOUNG PEOPLE near the main gate. The numbers have
increased.

She stands for some moments, a vast, lone figure.

ALISON COOPER walks past her on her way to the main gate.

MARTLETT turns and heads back towards the school.

Part Two

42   Int. Staircase. Day.   42

FIGG is walking up a very crowded staircase. MISS DENTON pushes her way through children to catch up with him.

> DENTON
> I hear you're making an anti-CP stand?

> FIGG
> Sorry . . . what was that?

> DENTON
> Corporal Punishment. I hear you've made a complaint about disruptives being sent to the Deputy Heads for discipline.

> FIGG
> No, I've not made a complaint. I just don't like kids wandering out of my class in my time to get their arses whacked.

> DENTON
> (cutting out of the stairway and through doorway)
> Whose time do you send yours in?

FIGG continues up the stairs.

43   Int. Corridor. Day.   43

TWENTYMAN and HODGESON are walking along a corridor on their way to their classrooms.

> HODGESON
> The whole class got high marks.

> TWENTYMAN
> That's good, isn't it?

HODGESON

But they knew the questions in advance.

TWENTYMAN

Yes, I know.

HODGESON

The whole purpose of a test is that the children do
not know what questions they are to be asked, so
they do not have an opportunity to prepare their
answers.

TWENTYMAN

Where else, other than at school, are they ever
going to be asked to do that?

HODGESON

In life, Mr Twentyman, in life! What is the point of
testing their general knowledge if they know the
questions in advance?

TWENTYMAN

So that they can approach and execute the task
without fear, without being marked down as
failures, so that they can research their work in
advance with the help and cooperation of people
around them. I mean, that's life as well, isn't it?

HODGESON

Mr Twentyman, in future, when a class is to be
tested –

TWENTYMAN moves off.

TWENTYMAN

I'm sorry, I'm late.

HODGESON

(following Twentyman)

I haven't finished, Mr Twentyman. Just one point.
Under no circumstances are you to teach
mammalian reproduction or sex education without
my permission, is that understood?

TWENTYMAN
If it comes up I can't avoid it. I follow what
interests the class.

HODGESON
(calling after him)
Our job, Mr Twentyman, is to follow the syllabus.
I stand by what I've said.

44   Ext. The garden. Day.   44

A new day.

A hot day. Short sleeves weather. Lunchtime.

The school garden plot, quite near the potting shed.
GRIFFITHS and FIGG are sitting on a couple of broken
classroom chairs against the wall of a small flat-roofed block
which houses workshops for metal work and carpentry and,
on the other side, Barratt's PE changing room.

GRIFFITHS and FIGG are looking out over the garden. As they
talk, they watch a group of BOYS making what looks to be a
kind of den and digging a trench which they attempt to fill
with water. TWENTYMAN comes out of the greenhouse
carrying three mugs of coffee.

Our visual attention is divided between the TEACHERS and
the construction work.

FIGG
I think I've got a classroom wanker.

GRIFFITHS
Stephen Harris – the one with the moustache –
known to his friends as Wanker Harris.

FIGG
No – he was at the front – Alan Fraser, a little lad
with blonde hair.

GRIFFITHS
Send the little bugger to me. Thank you.

On the flat roof: immediately above them, BARRATT is lying sunbathing. He is listening to the conversation.

GRIFFITHS
Geoff has got a wanker.

TWENTYMAN
Who?

GRIFFITHS
Little Alan Fraser – probably part of a gang.

FIGG
What do you mean?

GRIFFITHS
A wanking gang.

FIGG
What do you mean?

GRIFFITHS
They team up for mass wanking.

FIGG
In my class?

GRIFFITHS
Most likely. There's smoking gangs and glue gangs, there's randy gangs and wanking gangs . . .
(he looks at the boys)
What are they doing over there, that lot?

TWENTYMAN
They're constructing a motte-and-bailey Norman castle.

GRIFFITHS
Looks like pissing about to me. Hodgeson won't like it.

TWENTYMAN
I don't like what Hodgeson is doing to me, Vic.

GRIFFITHS does not respond.

TWENTYMAN
He's trying to teach me a lesson, Vic, put me in line. He doesn't like the way I teach.

GRIFFITHS
I don't want to get into this, but you're teaching mixed ability and it's getting up Hodgeson's nose. And others.

TWENTYMAN
Where do you stand, Vic?

GRIFFITHS
I don't take sides.

FIGG
What's the difference between a wanking gang and a randy gang?

GRIFFITHS
How glad I am you asked me that question. Wanking gangs sit around in groups ruining their eyesight – in the classroom. The whole point of a gang wank is to do it in the classroom. Mass desk tremor.

FIGG
And randy gangs?

GRIFFITHS
Randy gangs chase little girls around the playing field to get a smelly finger.

GRIFFITHS gets up.

TWENTYMAN
That's about the limit of sexual education in this school.

> GRIFFITHS
> The blind leading the blind.

The bell.

> GRIFFITHS
> What the hell's that? That bell's early!

GRIFFITHS scuttles off, the lunchbreak is over.

> FIGG
> Do you teach sex – to the kids, that is, in class?

> TWENTYMAN
> It's on the curriculum. They get a week of it in the
> second year.

> FIGG
> That's it?

> TWENTYMAN
> More or less. The 'details' are left to the parents.

> FIGG
> The blind leading the blind.

> TWENTYMAN
> They learn more from the lavatory walls than they
> do in a classroom.

> FIGG
> And nobody gives a toss. What do you do?

> TWENTYMAN
> I tell them everything. I'm writing them a book on
> it. We're on playground patrol tomorrow.

45	**Ext. Playground. Day.**	45

A new day.

FIGG and TWENTYMAN on playground patrol.

They are walking along the far side of a line of tennis courts.

The courts are full of PUPILS playing some kind of mass tennis – over thirty people to a court.

They pass STEPHEN HARRIS who is watching the action.

At one point, they put a stop to a minor scuffle.

46   Int. Corridor. Day.   46

The corridor outside VIC GRIFFITH's room.

Four assorted YOUTHS are waiting outside Griffith's door. Three 14–15-year-olds and PETER FIELD (12), a first year.

GRIFFITHS approaches along the corridor carrying a mug of coffee.

> GRIFFITHS
> What's wrong with Mr Kitchen's door?

Non-committal shrugs.

> YOUTH
> (with not much conviction)
> He's not there, sir.

> GRIFFITHS
> Neither was I, but you're here. Go to him for a change. Go on, sling your individual hooks . . .
> (to Field)
> What's your name?

> FIELD
> Peter Field, sir.

> GRIFFITHS
> I'll see you.

> OTHERS
> That's not fair, sir.

> GRIFFITHS
> That's right, it's not fair.

FIGG and TWENTYMAN see HARRIS push MILLS against a
wall and threaten him with a penknife.

> FIGG
> Look at that. Look at that bastard. I'll do it.

> TWENTYMAN
> (following)
> Don't hit him, whatever you do, don't hit him.

FIGG sprints down the staircase followed by TWENTYMAN
and out into the playground.

FIGG is angry. He grabs HARRIS.

> FIGG
> What are you doing? What's this? What the bloody
> hell do you think you're doing Harris?

> HARRIS
> Nothing, I ain't doing nothing.

> FIGG
> Give it.

> HARRIS
> What?

> FIGG
> Don't piss about – you know what. This!

He takes the knife.

> HARRIS
> What?

> FIGG
> This!
> (to Mills)
> He was threatening you, wasn't he?

HARRIS

I was doing nothing.

FIGG

You're a liar Harris. I watched you from that window.

HARRIS

So what – so what you going to do about it?

FIGG

Kick your arse is what I'd like to do.

HARRIS

You kick me and my dad'll be down here, I'll tell him. You can't do that.

FIGG

No, I can't, but I can send you to see Vic – no, not Vic, you go to see Mr Kitchen. You go to see Mr Kitchen. You wait outside his door. You wait, you hear, until he comes. And when he comes you tell him I sent you and you tell him what you were doing with this. You lie and I'll use it to cut off your balls. Now bugger off.

HARRIS
(as he goes)

I'll tell him you were swearing.

FIGG
(to Mills)

Don't worry, son, alright?

TWENTYMAN

Alright, Martin, you can go now. I'll talk to you later.

The staffroom is full.

FIGG takes a chair next to MISS DENTON.

> FIGG
> You'll be pleased to hear that I've just sent
> Stephen Harris of A4 to Mr Kitchen for using
> threatening behaviour.

> DENTON
> There's a collection going round for Mr Peters of
> the Geography Department, have you given
> anything?

> FIGG
> I don't know him, is he leaving?

> DENTON
> He's left –

> FIGG
> Oh.

> DENTON
> He died just before half term.

> FIGG
> I've only been here a few weeks, there are seventy
> staff, I've met twenty. I know seven. I just didn't
> get round to Mr Peters in time.

VIC GRIFFITHS leans over and breathes into FIGG's ear.

> GRIFFITHS
> Follow me.

50   Int. Vic's room/Corridor. Day.   50

Inside Griffith's room: STEPHEN HARRIS and MR GRANT, a
Geography teacher.

VIC and FIGG stride down the corridor and into the room.

>GRIFFITHS
>Ah, Geoff, great.

>FIGG
>(referring to Harris)
>What's he doing here? I sent him to Tony Kitchen.

>GRIFFITHS
>Did you now?

GRIFFITHS barrels out of the door:

51   Int. Corridor. Day.   51

>GRIFFITHS
>(steaming across the corridor)
>Stay there, Peter.

TWO BOYS are still standing outside Kitchen's door.

GRIFFITHS goes straight into Kitchen's office.

52   Int. Kitchen's office. Day.   52

>GRIFFITHS
>Will you do the honours on Stephen Harris, A4,
>extracting money with menaces? Refuses to bend
>over.

>KITCHEN
>Yes, of course.

The TWO MEN move out of the office into the corridor.

BARRATT is on his way down the corridor, accompanied by a BOY.

>GRIFFITHS
>Ah, Neal, thank you. I could do with a bit of muscle.

>BOY
>I got him for you, sir.

>GRIFFITHS
>Yes, I can see that, Brian, thank you very much. You can go now.
>(to Field)
>Not you.

FIVE TEACHERS and STEPHEN HARRIS.

>GRIFFITHS
>Stephen Harris, you are here because you are a bully and nobody in this school tolerates a bully, and that includes me – where's the knife?

>FIGG
>I've got it, Vic, here.

>HARRIS
>That's my knife.

>GRIFFITHS
>Shut up.
>(he opens the knife)
>Thank you. You were sent to Mr Kitchen but you came to see me, old softy Vic, but it doesn't matter because Mr Kitchen is here anyway. Look at that. You can kill with this, don't you know that? It's not a toy. It's a deadly weapon.

> HARRIS
> It's mine.

GRIFFITHS puts the knife in the drawer and takes out the slipper.

> GRIFFITHS
> You tell that to the police, Stephen. Now, I asked you nicely before these gentlemen arrived and now I'm going to ask you again. Will you please bend over?

> HARRIS
> No.

> GRIFFITHS
> OK, boys.

GRANT and BARRATT know why they're here, they grab at HARRIS's arms, KITCHEN goes for the slipper and GRIFFITHS goes for a leg.

A noisy, violent struggle ensues as HARRIS resists.

> GRIFFITHS
> Grab his leg, Geoff, get his other bloody leg.

FIGG dives in and takes a leg. Furniture is knocked over. Eventually, the FOUR MEN manage to straddle HARRIS across the table.

> GRIFFITHS
> OK . . . Tony . . .

KITCHEN proceeds to lay into HARRIS with considerable severity.

55   Int. Corridor. Day.   55

The corridor outside Vic's room.

FIELD is still waiting, listening to the noise in the room. He looks across the corridor to where the other two, older boys were standing. They have gone.

KITCHEN lays in to HARRIS with the last stroke out of six.

>   KITCHEN
> Finished.

The FOUR MEN let go of HARRIS, catch their breath, tuck in their shirts. KITCHEN is out of the door.

>   GRIFFITHS
> Thanks, boys.

BARRATT leaves without a word.

>   GRIFFITHS
> Okay, Stephen that's it. Nothing more to be said or done. You can go. Thanks, Gerry.

>   GRANT
> Any time, Vic.

GRANT leaves the office. HARRIS wipes his mouth, there is a small amount of blood. GRIFFITHS finds a tissue.

>   GRIFFITHS
> Here, wipe your mouth with that, it's not serious. See nurse, she'll put some Dettol on it.

HARRIS leaves the office.

FIGG is sitting on a chair, recovering.

A pause. GRIFFITHS tucks in his shirt.

>   GRIFFITHS
> Little bugger, look at that bloody knife.

>   FIGG
> Christ, Vic –

GRIFFITHS goes to the door.

>   GRIFFITHS
> Alright, Peter, in you come, boy.

PETER FIELD comes into the room. He is nervous, pale.

GRIFFITHS is still on a high but he tries to be gentle. He talks to the boy while making an entry in the punishment book.

When he has finished the entry he puts the book onto one side where it is picked up by FIGG, who looks through the entries while taking in the exchange between FIELD and GRIFFITHS.

> GRIFFITHS
> Now, Peter, what's it about, what are you here for, eh?

No reply.

> GRIFFITHS
> Who sent you?

> FIELD
> Mr James.

> GRIFFITHS
> What for?

No reply.

> GRIFFITHS
> Why did Mr James send you here, Peter?

> FIELD
> For . . . for making a noise . . . sir . . .

> GRIFFITHS
> What kind of noise were you making?

> FIELD
> A . . .
> (he makes a farting noise with his lips)
> sir . . .

> GRIFFITHS
> In class?

> FIELD
> Yes, sir.

GRIFFITHS
And did you make a
        (a farting noise)
noise in class?

FIELD
I don't know.

GRIFFITHS
You must know if you did or not; it's not the kind
of thing to escape one's notice, is it?

FIELD
I didn't mean to.

GRIFFITHS
But you did it?

FIELD
Yes, sir.

GRIFFITHS
So what's it going to be, Peter? You've not been to
me before, have you?

FIELD
No, sir.

GRIFFITHS
I can't give you lines 'I must not (noise) in class' a
thousand times. Writing should not be a
punishment. I can't keep you in detention, you're
too young. Do you want me to discuss it with your
mother and father?

FIELD
No, sir.

GRIFFITHS
So it has to be the slipper.

FIELD
I refuse the slipper, sir.

GRIFFITHS
Right.

Field's reply hits home, an unexpected response.

GRIFFITHS
. . . You have just said you refuse the slipper.

Silence.

GRIFFITHS
Is that correct?

FIELD
Yes, sir.

GRIFFITHS
Do you seriously want me to get in touch with
your mother and father?

FIELD
. . . No.

GRIFFITHS
It would mean writing a letter. They would have
to come down here. That would take time, and
you'd probably end up being whacked by the lot
of us. Do you want that?

FIELD
No, sir.

GRIFFITHS
Do you think you dad wants to take time off work
to discuss one little (makes a farting noise)?

FIELD
No, sir.

GRIFFITHS
Hell of a lot of trouble for one little (noise) isn't it?

FIELD
Yes, sir.

GRIFFITHS

So why not take the slipper?

FIELD

No, sir.

GRIFFITHS

It won't hurt. I won't hit you hard, promise. I'll
just give your bum one little tap and then you can
get back to your class and I can get back to
organising next year's timetable. OK?

FIELD

No, sir.

GRIFFITHS

Have you got something wrong with your bum?

FIELD

No.

GRIFFITHS

Then why don't you want the slipper?

FIELD

I don't have to have it, it says so in the staff
handbook.

GRIFFITHS

How do you know this, Peter?

FIELD

I read it in the staff handbook.

GRIFFITHS

Yes, but you're not staff, are you – are you?

FIELD

No, sir.

GRIFFITHS

Where did you find it?

FIELD

It was lying in the classroom, I read it.

The bell.

> FIGG
> Saved by the bell.

> GRIFFITHS
> No, this has to be solved.

> FIGG
> The bell has solved it, let him go.

> GRIFFITHS
> No. I can't.

> FIGG
> Give him a warning.

> GRIFFITHS
> I can't, alright?

> FIGG
> Why not?

> GRIFFITHS
> You can see what happens if you let them get
> away with it. You treat them soft, they think
> you're soft. It has to be sorted out. It's my job.

> FIGG
> Look at him, Vic.

> GRIFFITHS
> If he doesn't want the slipper I shall have to
> contact his parents. Those are the rules, I didn't
> make them. Now, Peter, I want you to wait here
> and think about it, and all the long time I am away
> I want you to think about what you are doing, and
> when I come back we will discuss it again.

GRIFFITHS leaves the office. FIGG slides the punishment book
into his plastic carrier bag and follows VIC.

End shot on FIELD.

Barratt's private changing room.

Rear view as BARRATT takes off his trousers and underpants in one manoeuvre. As he stands up, we see that on his open locker door there are two or three colour photographs of female nudes in open crutch poses.

MALE NUDE checks out the female nudes and then checks out himself, just to make sure that God really did give him the biggest penis in the world.

He reaches for his jock strap to put it on.

GRIFFITHS and FIGG proceed along their usual route which leads to the block which houses the Chemistry lab.

From a window on the third floor, STEPHEN HARRIS looks down on the TWO MEN and watches their progress across the open area. VIC is in a black mood.

>   GRIFFITHS
> By the time he reaches the third year he'll be a
> spotty yob just like Stephen Harris.
>
>   FIGG
> Rubbish. The kid has potential.
>
>   GRIFFITHS
> You'd have said that about Harris when he was
> twelve, but now you've got him marked down as
> thick, just like the rest of us.
>   (yells at some children)
> The bell has gone, get to your classrooms!
> 'Potential' is standing around this school smoking
> Silk Cut and hating our guts. And I have devoted
> my life to them. You have entered an educational
> waste land where the fertile soil of intelligence
> ends and the desert of ignorance begins.

Four ropes hang from the ceiling, mats on the floor.

FOUR BOYS, including ALAN FRASER, are climbing up the ropes. They all find it hard going. FRASER is anything but the slowest person in the class.

A blast from BARRATT's whistle. The FOUR BOYS slither down the ropes and drop to the ground.
BARRATT has a pair of boxing gloves round his neck. FRASER hits the floor, BARRATT blasts on the whistle for silence.

>   BARRATT
> . . . Quiet!

He moves over to FRASER. A BOY in one of the lines speaks to ANOTHER BOY.

>   BARRATT
> I mean quiet, Claxton, right?
>   (to Fraser)
> Hold out your hands.

He shoves the boxing gloves onto FRASER's hands. He raises FRASER's hands into the air and walks round him. Fraser slackens his arms but BARRATT pulls them into the air again.

>   BARRATT
> Fraser wears the gloves in gym and on the playing
> fields until he has the strength to reach the roof.
>   (in close to Fraser, quiet)
> And you should wear them at home in bed,
> Fraser, then you'd stop fiddling with your
> disgusting, smelly little winkle. You wanker!

60   **Int. Vic's room. Day.**   **60**

PETER FIELD stands alone, isolated in the centre of the room, head down.

School noises echo in the distance.

MARTLETT is at her desk and there is a TYPIST at work.
TWENTYMAN is using the photostat machine.

A knock on the door, FIGG comes into the office.

> FIGG
> Hello . . .

> MARTLETT
> Yes, can I help you, Mr Figg?

> FIGG
> I'd like to use the stat machine, if that's OK . . . ?

> MARTLETT
> It's in use at the moment.

> FIGG
> . . . Right.

> TWENTYMAN
> I've finished.

TWENTYMAN collects up his papers. He drops one.
ELIZABETH MARTLETT notices it as there is another knock on
the door and HODGESON comes into the office. MARTLETT
picks up the paper dropped by TWENTYMAN, but does not
return it to him.

> MARTLETT
> Ah, I'll tell Mr Griff you're here, Mr Hodgeson.

TWENTYMAN is on his way out of the office. HODGESON
follows him.

In the corridor:

> HODGESON
> Mr Twentyman.

> TWENTYMAN
> Mr Hodgeson.

>   HODGESON
> Aren't you with B3?

>   TWENTYMAN
> Yes.

>   HODGESON
> I've just seen six boys parading with no
> supervision across the garden with forks over their
> shoulders, several are wandering aimlessly about
> the grounds –

>   TWENTYMAN
> They're collecting feathers.

>   HODGESON
> – the rest are in the classroom and you are here.

>   MARTLETT
> Mr Hodgeson.

TWENTYMAN walks off down the corridor. HODGESON goes into Griff's study.

We stay with FIGG to see that he is copying the punishment book.

MARTLETT comes back into the office.

>   FIGG
> Miss Martlett, I'd like to see Mr Griff.

>   MARTLETT
> . . . Oh . . .

>   FIGG
>   (bright)
> Can you fix it for me please?

>   MARTLETT
> . . . It'll mean a wait.

>   FIGG
> Great. Fine. Terrific.

He smiles, prepared to wait all day, as copies of pages from the punishment book roll off the photostat machine.

62	**Int. Griff's study. Day.**	62

> GRIFF
> You came into teaching late, didn't you? You've only been at it a couple of terms.

> FIGG
> What's that got to do with it?

> GRIFF
> This school is not the brightest star in the educational firmament, Mr Figg, we have less than the borough's share of able pupils. That's why I took you . . . and your first class degree. We need first class teachers.
> (he picks up the copy of the letter Figg has
> given him, shakes his head)
> If you want to raise some issues there are more important ones than this.

63	**Ext. Main gate. Day.**	63

End of the day. The tarmac driveway leading to the main gate.

GRIFFITHS is one of the last out of the school. He carries an old, over-laden briefcase and a rolled up sheet of paper which is the master plan for next year's timetable.

FIGG catches up with him.

> FIGG
> I've been wanting to return this library book.
> (the punishment book)

> GRIFFITHS
> It's long overdue. I noted that it had gone missing from the shelves.

> FIGG
> Books like this shouldn't be on the shelves.

> GRIFFITHS
> It's there for all to see – as you have discovered.

> FIGG
> It's pornographic.

GRIFFITHS stops so as to open his briefcase.

> GRIFFITHS
> A catalogue of crime.

> FIGG
> Petty misdemeanours. *Boys' Own* stuff.
> (he reads)
> 'Fooling on sports – 1'
> 'Out of bounds – 1'

The noise of a hooter. They move out of the way so that
MARTLETT can drive through in her Mini.

> GRIFFITHS
> I'd like to give her one, you know, right there in
> the front seat.

> FIGG
> (reads)
> 'Nuisance in assembly – 2 strokes of the slipper',
> 'Bullying', 'Late', 'General nuisance', 'Jeans and
> still no note'. Hitting kids for that.

> GRIFFITHS
> (takes the book and stuffs it into his briefcase)
> Don't moan at me, see Griff.

They walk on and out of the main gate.

> FIGG
> I have. Told him I was sick in the gut for sending
> Harris to be beaten.

> GRIFFITHS
> What did he say?

FIGG

Everyone pukes when they kill their first German.
Then I put in a complaint about the excessive use
of corporal punishment in the school. Official. In
writing – with a copy to the Education Office.

GRIFFITHS

You've done that?

FIGG

I have.

GRIFFITHS

Quick work.

FIGG

Right.

GRIFFITHS

It won't do you any good.

FIGG

That's what he said.

GRIFFITHS

If you're going to start stirring, Geoff, I don't want
to know.

FIGG

Little Peter Field, what happened?

GRIFFITHS

He came round to my way of thinking.

FIGG

. . . Great.

GRIFFITHS

I've got better things to do than write letters
about farts.

WHITAKER, the Bursar, and a CARETAKER, shut and lock the
school gates. The YOUNG PEOPLE are still hanging around at
the gates. Some of them grab a free ride on the gate as it is
closed. WHITAKER is a target; they enjoy mocking him.

Part Three

64   **Ext. School car park. Day.**   **64**

Some days later.

Head down, with three newspapers under his arm, GRIFF
gets out of his car and heads towards the school.

Behind GRIFF, WHITAKER (the Bursar, a retired military man)
canters to catch up with him. WHITAKER is in something of a
fury; he is brandishing a newspaper.

> WHITAKER
> . . . Mr Griff . . .
>> (shaking the newspaper as if it was human)
> There . . .
>> (he proceeds to tear the newspaper into
>> shreds)
> That . . . that . . . is . . . what . . . I . . . think
> . . . of that!

In the background, MARTLETT pulls up in her Mini and
clambers swiftly out of the driving seat (impossible). She is
holding two newspapers.

> WHITAKER
>> (stuffing the newspaper into a waste bin)
> I've taken that newspaper for thirty-eight years.

> GRIFF
>> (walking on into the school)
> Yes. Thank you, Mr Whitaker.

> MARTLETT
>> (waving her newspaper)
> Mr Griff . . . Mr Griff!

GRIFF is bright but somewhat tense.

> MARTLETT
> There have been two calls from the press and
> twenty-three from parents pledging their support.

> GRIFF
> Nothing is to be done about Mr Figg, not yet. Book
> me a call to the Chief Education Officer. I will not
> have time to speak to any newspaper reporters.
> Those people in the office, are they for me?

> MARTLETT
> No. Unscheduled visitors.

> GRIFF
> Ex-pupils?

> MARTLETT
> Yes – I've told them that –

> GRIFF
> Bring them in.

MARTLETT does not consider this to be wise.

> GRIFF
> In spite of what is to be read in the newspapers,
> Elizabeth, today is a normal day. Business as
> usual. Bring them in.

A4 move into the classroom where FIGG is waiting, sitting on
the desk.

FIGG has re-arranged the classroom: the desks are at the back
of the room and the chairs in a semi-circle towards the front
of the room.

A lot of noise as the PUPILS come into the classroom, questions and wisecracks about the newspapers and reactions to the new furniture arrangements.

> PUPILS
> Oi oi! / Have you seen your name in the paper, sir? / Have you seen the paper? / Wass all this? / We ain't got no desks. / They been stuck up the back. / Oi, sir, can I have your autograph? / You famous? / You gonna be on the tele? / Oi, sir, somebody's messed up all the chairs.

> SYLVE
> Have you seen the paper, sir? Have you seen it?

> FIGG
> Yes, Sylve, I have.

> SYLVE
> Did you do that?

> FIGG
> Yes, I did.

> SYLVE
> What a bloody silly thing to do. What's the point? That won't get you nowhere.

Some of the BOYS have started to drag the desks to the front of the class.

> FIGG
> Hold it! Leave it – put that table back exactly where it was. Sit down. Right. This is a subject I want to raise.
> (he starts to write on the blackboard)
> It isn't unemployment. It isn't unidentified flying objects. It isn't plastic grass.

He has written the word 'MASTURBATION' on the blackboard. Silence. Confusion. A considerable number of the class do not know what it means, some cannot read it. They look to each other for information.

FIGG

Some of you may not know what that word means
so here's another one which means the same thing.

As the meaning is whispered round the class and is greeted
with incredulous gasps, FIGG writes the word 'WANKING'
up on the board. Sensation.

67   Int. Griff's study. Day.   67

There are THREE YOUNG PEOPLE with GRIFF.

BARRY (16) covered in acne, wearing a thick pullover, no
shirt, cord jeans and plimsolls. White.

DAWN (nearly 17) wearing a long leather coat. Black.

PAUL (nearly 18) very well built, very fit. Black.

> GRIFF
> (his mind is elsewhere)
> And how has it been going, Paul?

> PAUL
> I'm Paul.

> BARRY
> I'm Barry.

> GRIFF
> Yes, what have you been up to since you left,
> Barry? When did you leave?

> BARRY
> Last term.

> GRIFF
> An Easter leaver.

> BARRY
> Yes, sir.

> GRIFF
> And what about you, Dawn?

                    BARRY
I didn't tell you what I've been doing.

                    GRIFF
I was going to come back to you, Paul, but do tell
me.

                    BARRY
I got a job as soon as I left.

                    GRIFF
Good. Where?

                    BARRY
The abattoir.

                    GRIFF
And how's that going?

                    BARRY
I left, ain't got nothing now.

                    GRIFF
You left. Not dismissed?

                    BARRY
No.

                    GRIFF
Why did you leave?

                    BARRY
I liked the work but I couldn't get on with the
people.

68   Int. Classroom. Day.   68

As a subject heading at the top of the blackboard FIGG has
written 'SEX'. Next to 'WANKING' FIGG has written 'IN
CLASS'.

                    FIGG
A show of hands, those in favour, raise their
hands.

No show of hands.

>FIGG
>No votes for. Those against, please raise their hands.

Almost half the class put up their hands, a majority of GIRLS. A lot of BOYS are still sitting looking guarded, suspicious.

>FIGG
>OK, at least half the class votes against, the rest are abstentions. That means the class votes against masturbation in the classroom during lessons. If you had a vote and didn't use it, it doesn't count. That's democracy.

>RAMKISSOON
>That's not fair.

>FIGG
>Why not?

>RAMKISSOON
>Most of those who stuck their hands up were girls.

>FIGG
>Why's that not fair, Feisal?

>BLUNT
>They don't do it, do they?

Guffaws from the BOYS.

>FIGG
>Girls can masturbate just the same as boys. I'll explain with a diagram. While I'm doing that, here's a box with some pieces of paper in it.
>(he hands out little squares of paper)
>Take a piece of paper out of the box, write down any question about sex that you want. Fold it over and put it back in the box. I promise I will answer it. Here's your chance to find out where you came from.

69   Int. Martlett's office. Day.   69

Three more YOUTHS from the gate are in MARTLETT's office.
MARTLETT and SECRETARY present.

TERRY has *slight* difficulty in keeping a straight face.

> TERRY
> This is George and this is George. Two Georges.
> And I'm Terry.

> MARTLETT
> And what can I do for you?

> TERRY
> We came to see Mr Griff . . . . . . say 'ello, like.

70   Int. Griff's study/Corridor. Day.   70

> PAUL
> At first it was a bit hard not having any O levels
> and only one CSE. I had to take anything that
> come my way, but then I got a lucky break and
> landed this job with a computer firm. I'm doing
> very nicely thank you very much.

> GRIFF
> Good.

> PAUL
> Raking it in.

DAWN laughs.

> GRIFF
> And the suit you are wearing was supplied by the
> computer firm.

> PAUL
> Yeah, do you like it?

GRIFF
(getting up)
This is not funny.

BARRY
This is not funny!

GRIFF goes to his study door and calls to WHITAKER who is trying to get rid of GEORGE, GEORGE and TERRY.

GRIFF
Elizabeth – Ah, Mr Whitaker, come in a moment, please. Mr Whitaker will you see these young people off the premises? You are not funny. I don't have time to waste. If you are seen on school property again, the police will be called.

BARRY makes the noise of a police siren.

GEORGE
(overlap with Griff and Whitaker)
Oi, Barry, what you doing in there?

BARRY
Having a nice cup of coffee.

GRIFF
Mr Whitaker, please see these young people off the school premises.

WHITAKER
Yes, Mr Griff. Come on.

GRIFF
I suggest less time hanging around street corners and more time smartening yourselves up and tracking down a job.

BARRY
Bollocks!

PAUL
Yeah.

DAWN
(quiet)
Old pratt.

WHITAKER
None of that – out.

BARRY
Bursar Ben, the Flower Pot Man.

PAUL lets out a very loud belch. GEORGE, GEORGE and
TERRY hear him and let off a few more.

WHITAKER
Less of your lip, come on.

GRIFF
Any trouble and the police will be called.

They are moving out of the study and along the corridor.
GRIFF is angry. Dialogue overlaps.

DAWN
(above all the rest)
I been out of school a year and I done nothing.

GRIFF
Please leave peacefully.

DAWN
I bin for one job and they didn't want me cos I'm
black.

MARTLETT
This will be reported –

DAWN
Shut up, you fat old cow.

WHITAKER
Enough of that.

TERRY
(sing song)
Bristol City . . . . .

Burps from GEORGE and GEORGE.

>   MARTLETT
> I know your names –

>   DAWN
> The Incredible Bulk – that's your bleedin name.

>   WHITAKER
> Out! Out.

>   BARRY
>   (calling back)
> Up your arse, Griff!

>   PAUL
> Rhas clat – honky!

>   BARRY
> Whey hey!

>   TERRY
> Bristol Cities . . .

>   ALL TOGETHER
>   (chant)
> Bristol Cities, Great big titties! Oi!

---

71   **Int. Classroom. Day.**   **71**

On the blackboard is a drawing of the vagina showing the clitoris.

FIGG takes questions out of the box.

>   FIGG
> Right, we'll start by reading out all the questions
> and then I'll go through them one by one, and
> give you my answers.
>   (he reads)
> 'Why have I got balls and girls don't?' That's a
> good question, I presume it comes from a boy.
> 'What are rags?' 'Is wanking wrong? Is it bad for

me?' The answer is no, but I'll come back to it. 'What is the pox?' 'Where do you . . .' what's this? 'Where do you get love juice?' 'Where do you get love juice?' 'Do you wank?' Yes, I do. 'Have you had VD?' Yes, I have, but there are different sorts and I'll tell you what I know. 'Do homos kiss? Are you a homo if you kiss?' I think I know what that means. 'Why do boys get the horn?'

>PUPILS
Eh? What?

>FIGG
The horn is a way of describing the penis when it becomes stiff. It is usually called an 'erection'.

A gasp from SYLVE.

>FIGG
What is it, Sylve?

>SYLVE
(covering her ignorance)
Nothing.

>FIGG
(reads)
'Is fuck a swear word?'

72   Int. Corridor. Day.   72

FIGG walks along a corridor towards Twentyman's Rural Studies room.

The sound of Jelly Roll Morton and his Red Hot Peppers playing 'Smoke House Blues' can be heard drifting down the corridor.

73   Int. Rural Studies room. Day.   73

TWENTYMAN's Rural Studies room.

TWENTYMAN is sitting with his feet up, listening to the music. He is drinking a cup of tea and there is a CAT asleep on his lap. FIGG appears in the doorway.

> FIGG
> Any chance of a cup of tea for a staffroom refugee, brother?

> TWENTYMAN
> On the stove.

FIGG pours himself a cup of tea from the tea pot on the stove.

> FIGG
> I've just had sex with A4 during Religious Instruction. Revelation upon revelation.

> TWENTYMAN
> The blind leading the blind.

> FIGG
> Hungry for knowledge. You can see the relief on their faces.

As they talk, FIGG looks at the rich variety of material to be found in the classroom There are many books and magazines. On the walls and around the classroom are signs of projects which individual children have taken up. Some of them do not necessarily relate directly to Rural Studies, such as pictures of a jump jet, a motte-and-bailey Norman castle, science fiction posters.

On the walls: a combination of photographs taken by the children, cut from magazines, newspapers, books; drawings, paintings, maps, plans and written work all carried out by the children.

Topics include: birds – their nests, eggs and how the young chick develops inside the egg. Next to these pictures are Lennart Nilsson's remarkable pictures of the development of the foetus inside the womb. Pick up on a picture of Jane Twentyman showing her bare, pregnant tummy.

There are diagrams of how birds fly. Next to this, the skeleton of a bird. Their food. Pictures of the largest and the smallest birds in the world.

How things grow: vegetables, plants, trees, including a section of a tree showing the root system.

The life cycle: birth, childhood, youth and adolescence, adulthood, old age, death.

There are photographs of the different classes taken by the pupils during the lessons. Some of these are happy group pictures with TWENTYMAN in the centre of the picture, laughing, surrounded by happy people.

There are plants and animals in the classroom; a JACKDAW, a BROWN RAT, a couple of RABBITS and the CAT.

There are pictures of the animals and plants that we eat showing all the various additives, such as hormones and chemicals, which are used in the growing of these foods and are a danger to health. There are similar charts relating to fast foods – all carried out by the children and displayed and made available in the classroom for general use.

There is a large collection of objects: an animal gintrap, a bow and arrow, a washing dolly, an old radio, a new radio, various old tools, etc. There is a practical cooker and a portable gramophone with a collection of records. A tape recorder, typewriter, slide projector and a camera.

And more.

FIGG takes in the classroom.

>   FIGG
> How do you get away with it?

>   TWENTYMAN
> With difficulty.

>   FIGG
> Have you read the papers?

TWENTYMAN
Who's your mole?

FIGG
No mole. I took the punishment book out of Vic's
office, made copies, rang the paper, sent them off.
I got a card from the staff.

FIGG takes out a card with a piece of chalk stuck to it.

FIGG
(reads)
'The British Confraternity of Teachers. The Broken
Piece of Chalk Award presented to Geoffrey Figg
for the finest example of gross unprofessional
conduct.' Where's the bin?

TWENTYMAN
Find a space. Put it on the wall.

FIGG
What for?

TWENTYMAN
Open classroom. Let them see what's going on.

FIGG finds a space and pins the card up on the wall.

FIGG
There's a funny smell. Who cleans this lot?

TWENTYMAN
We do. The cleaners help out. They like coming in
here.

FIGG
(looking at the work displayed)
How do you get them to do all this?

TWENTYMAN
They do it.

FIGG
They wouldn't do it if you weren't here to make
them do it, though, would they?

TWENTYMAN
It happens because I let it happen.

FIGG
You just sit there with your fingers up your nose.

TWENTYMAN
No. I usually make them tell me what they're
going to do, but they choose.

FIGG looks round the classroom in silence. He finds the
remains of a rabbit, somewhat crudely dissected.

FIGG
What's this?

TWENTYMAN
Dissection.

FIGG
Looks like the rudiments of murder.

TWENTYMAN
We're going to cook it.

FIGG
Good luck.

FIGG continues his tour.

FIGG
It's great. How do you do it?

TWENTYMAN
Authority and discipline. Tie their hands behind
their backs and stuff it down their throats.

FIGG
What's the answer?

TWENTYMAN
(referring to his classroom)
My answer – this. 'Love is fitter than fear,
gentleness better than beating, to bring up a child
rightly in learning' . . . and if that doesn't work,
clout the bastards round the ear.

FIGG
What happens to the cat at weekends?

TWENTYMAN
It goes home like the rest of us, with Lynda Butt in
B3.

74   Ext. The gate. Day.   74

MARTLETT and WHITAKER contemplate the large gathering
of YOUNG PEOPLE at the gate, some of whom are standing
on the gate, whistling and looking at WHITAKER and
MARTLETT. There is nothing threatening about their
behaviour. TERRY rides forwards on his motorbike and gives
the 'V' sign to WHITAKER and MARTLETT. Cheers and
applause.

WHITAKER
What's it to be then?

MARTLETT
Make another appeal to them to go away, then we
call in the police to disperse them.

WHITAKER
You'd better get clearance for that, Elizabeth.

MARTLETT
. . . Very well.

They walk back towards the school.

75   Int. Griff's study. Day.   75

GRIFF
You have continued to deal with mammalian
reproduction and sex education.

TWENTYMAN
I have not set out with the intention of dealing
with those subjects.

GRIFF
Yes, but do you teach them?

TWENTYMAN
I answer their questions. The time allowed on the syllabus does not match their curiosity. Next term, I'm down to teach the second years, I shall allow them the time they need.

GRIFF
You will not be required to teach this subject next term, Mr Twentyman.

TWENTYMAN
(pulled up)
Why not?

GRIFF produces the paper dropped by TWENTYMAN in the office.

GRIFF
I believe this belongs to you.

TWENTYMAN sees the paper but does not react.

GRIFF
(reads)
'What is an orgasm?' 'What is cunnilingus?' 'How do homosexuals make love?' I must confess that . .
(he shakes his head)
. . . it's . . . a whole series of questions with detailed, graphic answers. And this page, I presume, is a part of a whole series of pages, is that correct?

TWENTYMAN
That's right.

GRIFF
And you have introduced this material into the classroom?

TWENTYMAN
That's right.

GRIFF
For what age groups?

TWENTYMAN
For those who are interested.

GRIFF
Boys and girls.

TWENTYMAN
Boys and girls.

GRIFF
Of any age.

TWENTYMAN
Of any age.

GRIFF
This is appalling, without decency. I am deeply shocked.

GRIFF opens a drawer in his desk and takes out a book called *Open Sex, Open Mind*.

GRIFF
Do you recognise that?

TWENTYMAN
Yes.

GRIFF
This book was confiscated from boys in the Science laboratory after one of your lessons. This is a very grave situation Mr Twentyman.

TWENTYMAN
I see.

TWENTYMAN takes a magazine from his briefcase. The title of the magazine is *Phoenix*.

TWENTYMAN
Take a look at that.

GRIFF
Good God.

TWENTYMAN
Take a look.

GRIFF
I don't think I want to look.

TWENTYMAN flicks through the magazine for GRIFF's benefit. It shows pictures of young women dressed as school girls displaying their spanked bottoms.

TWENTYMAN
This is a spanking magazine: it caters for people who derive sexual excitement from caning and spanking. With titles like 'Over Teacher's Knee' I leave it to you to divine the cause. I bought it this morning from the local newsagents, after reading our publicity. I copied that
(the paper)
from that – it's a school library book.

GRIFF
I beg your pardon?

TWENTYMAN
I borrowed that the day it came into the school library. I made my own edited version when I was asked to return it. I thought it had gone missing.

GRIFF moves back to the magazine.

GRIFF
Have you shown this to children in the school?

TWENTYMAN
No, no, no, that is not why I bought it, but we're a spanking school, why not show them? Avail them of some of the fringe benefits.

> GRIFF
>
> This is dragging us all into deeper water, Mr
> Twentyman. Here is a paper setting out twelve
> conditions regarding your teaching in this school.
> They include abandoning your *laissez-faire* system
> of teaching in favour of a disciplined structure to
> be administered by Mr Hodgeson. The curriculum
> and the syllabus are there to be adhered to. You
> are to follow Mr Hodgeson's instructions.

76	**Int. Corridor. Day.**	**76**

The corridor outside Griff's study.

FIGG is waiting in the corridor. TWENTYMAN comes out of
the study. MARTLETT looms large in the background.

> FIGG
> How many did you get?

> TWENTYMAN
> Six on each knuckle.

The bell.

TWENTYMAN walks off down the corridor. ALISON COOPER
is waiting for her appointment with Griff.

> FIGG
> Me now, is it?

> MARTLETT
> Yes, Mr Figg. Oh, Mr Twentyman, your wife has
> been taken into hospital.

FIGG hears this as he goes into the office and through into
Griff's study. MR WHITAKER – Bursar Ben – is in the office.

> MARTLETT
> Yes, can I help you?

> COOPER
> I have –

                    TWENTYMAN
When?

                    MARTLETT
They telephoned a few minutes ago.

                    TWENTYMAN
When did she go into labour?

                    MARTLETT
They did not say.

                    TWENTYMAN
I must go.

                    MARTLETT
You have classes . . .

                    TWENTYMAN
(looks at his watch)
I am leaving in forty minutes, at the end of my
next class. Thank you for telling me.

He walks off down the corridor.

                    MARTLETT
(to Cooper)
Yes, you were saying?

                    COOPER
I have an appointment with Mr Griff. Alison
Cooper.

                    MARTLETT
Alison. Yes. You're going to have to wait.

                    COOPER
I don't mind.

MARTLETT goes into the office and closes the door. COOPER
stands in the corridor, prepared for a long wait.

| 77 | **Int. Vic's room. Day.** | 77 |

The door is closed.

GRIFFITHS, smoking a Gold Flake, looks at the chart. It is complete: classroom allocations, etc., are filled in and groups and streams indicated by coloured arrows and dots.

Job satisfaction at having completed a complex task.

The bell, which carries over into:

| 78 | **Int. Laboratory/Corridor. Day.** | 78 |

Empty third-floor corridor – the bell is still ringing.

TWENTYMAN, having grabbed his briefcase, is the first one out of the laboratory. He sprints off down the corridor.

B1 – 12-YEAR-OLDS – make their way out of the lab.

| 79 | **Int. Classroom. Day.** | 79 |

A classroom on the ground floor.

A4 make their way out of the classroom. STEPHEN HARRIS cuts out of the main stream of people and heads towards the fire exit leading to the back stairs.

| 80 | **Ext. Playground. Day.** | 80 |

VIC GRIFFITHS is leaving his office to teach a class, taking the usual route to the Chemistry lab block.

He meets FIGG and they walk along together.

FIGG has *not* got his plastic carrier bag.

> GRIFFITHS
> Well?

> FIGG
> Red card job.

> GRIFFITHS
> Has he sent you off?

> FIGG
> Not yet, but he's talking about suspension.

> GRIFFITHS
> Stupid. You, I mean. There are procedures, professional procedures. You could have made an official complaint.

> FIGG
> Would it have made any difference?

> GRIFFITHS
> They'll nail your arse to the wall.

81   Int. Stairs/Corridor/Laboratory. Day.   81

HARRIS hits the top of the stairs, through the fire exit, along the corridor to the Chemistry lab. He smashes open the door into the lab, moving at speed. He grabs several large jars of chemicals and piles them onto a tray. He goes over to the window and opens it.

He looks down to see GRIFFITHS and FIGG coming out of the main building to make their way across to the block.

82   Ext. Playground. Day.   82

GRIFFITHS and FIGG on the way past the tennis courts.

> FIGG
> I've stirred things up, people know about it now.

> GRIFFITHS
> He's going to put a ban on corporal punishment.

This is a blow to FIGG.

> FIGG
> What?

GRIFFITHS

Griff told me himself. Homage to Strasbourg.
Phase it out over the next two years.

FIGG

That's points to me.

GRIFFITHS

He's going to throw the whole question of
discipline right back at the parents – do you think
they're going to thank you for that?

FIGG

It'll still look like a victory to me.

GRIFFITHS
(stops, angry)

What? What was that word? You think you're
going to turn the entire system onto its head? One
and a half terms in the profession – Johnny-come-
lately – and you talk about victories? Here, in here,
golden rule number one, the only rule: Get
Through The Day. And that's it. There are no
victories, boy.

FIGG

I've stirred things up, Vic.

GRIFFITHS
(shakes his head)

A mere ripple. You're on the wrong side of too
many people, Brother Figg. Go public. Apologise
to Griff –

FIGG

What?

GRIFFITHS

Apologise to the *Headmaster* – or you'll be out on
your arse. No reference and no pension.

> FIGG
> (stops)
> Ahhh, shit. I've left my bag in the Bulk's office.

FIGG turns to go back to Martlett's office.

> FIGG
> (over his shoulder)
> Have I got to apologise to her as well?

GRIFFITHS continues towards the block.

As FIGG reaches the door of the main block, there is a crash. Jars of chemicals and broken glass shower down on GRIFFITHS from the fourth floor.

The glass glitters in the sun as it falls.

83	**Int. Laboratory. Day.**	83

HARRIS, having tipped the tray of chemicals out of the window, throws a laboratory stool at the window, breaking the glass.

84	**Ext. Playground. Day.**	84

FIGG runs towards GRIFFITHS to help him. Two or three OTHER PEOPLE appear and run to where GRIFFITHS is lying on the ground, badly injured by the glass and chemicals.

85	**Int. Corridor. Day.**	85

The corridor outside the Science lab.

HARRIS cuts out of the Science lab and along the corridor to the fire exit.

As he goes through the door, HODGESON and some PUPILS come through the door at the other end of the corridor. HARRIS has escaped without detection.

FIGG sits on a bench in the Casualty Department of the local
hospital. He has been considerably shaken by the event; after
all, he was almost the victim of this seemingly mindless act of
violence.

87   **Int. Corridor. Day.**   **87**

The corridor outside Griff's study. GRIFF comes out of
MARTLETT's office. There are POLICEMEN in the office.

>   GRIFF
> There's been a terrible accident – you probably
> heard the sirens . . .

>   COOPER
> Yes.

>   GRIFF
> We have the police in – but, business as usual.
> You've waited all afternoon, Alison, it must be
> important.

88   **Ext. Hospital Corridor. Day.**   **88**

FIGG stands at the centre of a four-way intersection. Another
factory.
He is searching for the maternity ward.

89   **Int. Griff's study. Day.**   **89**

>   COOPER
> And I've done two more A levels since I left
> school.

>   GRIFF
> So you've got a healthy clutch of O and A levels.
> You deserve a rest.

COOPER
I'm going to have one.

GRIFF
Good. Where are you going?

COOPER
To sign on the dole.

GRIFF
(laughs)
Oh . . . I see. Really? Not for long, I'll be bound.

COOPER
That's really not up to me, is it, Mr Griff?

GRIFF
Take a rest, think about it. You can't expect it all to happen immediately. But you do have certain advantages over your friends, Alison. You come from a good home, and you have a healthy display of qualifications, extremely healthy – did you get Maths?

COOPER
Yes.

GRIFF
Well done. A head for figures.

COOPER
I did what you wanted. I did as I was told. I learned what I was told to learn and reproduced it on paper, the way you wanted it.

GRIFF
Yes . . . ?

COOPER
So what happens now?

GRIFF
It's up to you. You have to get out and do things for yourself.

COOPER

How do you do that? You never taught us that.
You taught us to rely on you. No work – now. No
work – ever. What have you done to help us live
with that?

GRIFF

Don't rely on us, rely on yourself. We gave you an
education, we gave you qualifications – what more
do you want? It's up to you what you do with it.
There are twelve hundred children in this school
and over seventy staff. What do you expect?
Teaching *you* was a pleasure. *You* are not a
problem. You are a *success*.

COOPER
(taking documents out of her bag)
These are my O level certificates. These are my A
levels – this is why I came here today – I would
like you to roll them up and to push them up your
arse. Oh, yes, and there's this.

She takes a silver plated trophy from her bag.

COOPER
You can stuff this too.

Pause.

GRIFF
(hurt, deeply disappointed)
Why use language like that?

| 90 | **Int. Hospital corridor. Day.** | 90 |

A hospital corridor near the maternity ward.

FIGG and TWENTYMAN sit together.

FIGG
They're patching him up. Told me to go back in an
hour. How was the birth?

>   TWENTYMAN
> A tribute to pethidine. Wife looked like she'd got
> flu. Baby was prised out like a limp fish and
> looked hung over. At the last minute a gang of
> medical students came in. I had to fight to get a
> view.
>> (he laughs, thinks of his wife and baby and
>> begins to cry)

91   Ext. Playground. Day.   91

There is a police car in the playground.

WHITAKER is in a confrontation with the CROWD at the gate. He is trying to stop them from climbing onto the gate. He has ordered them to disperse.

>   WHITAKER
>   (shouts)
> Five minutes!

>   CROWD
> Bollocks!

The bell for the end of the day sounds.

>   WHITAKER
> Ignorant bloody hooligans.

On her way out of the school, ALISON COOPER picks a trophy shield from the wall, walks outside, and throws it through a window. Cheers from the CROWD.

WHITAKER tries to apprehend COOPER as she runs towards the gate. The CROWD boos at him and starts to throw missiles such as cans, bottles and stones. WHITAKER retreats towards school. The CROWD chases him, throwing things as they go.

As WHITAKER reaches the school entrance, TWO POLICEMEN are on their way out. They attract further abuse and missiles. They try to run to their car but are beaten back. The CROWD attacks the car.

Panic inside the school. 1,200 PUPILS are leaving their classrooms at the end of the day.

HODGESON is running down the corridor shouting instructions. Other TEACHERS run past him to reach other parts of the school.

HODGESON opens a classroom door.

> HODGESON
> Back! Back! Back into your classrooms! And walk! Walk! Mrs Denton, stay in your classroom! The children must not leave!

A corridor: the boys' lavatory and cloakrooms on the one side, a window looking out onto the playground and main entrance on the other.

A POLICEMAN runs down the corridor shouting to a group of FIRST YEAR CHILDREN who are confused and do not know what to do.

> POLICEMAN
> Back into your classrooms! This is an emergency – please stay in your classrooms!

Stones thrown from outside splatter against the windows which crack and begin to break. Panic. The POLICEMAN goes for the door nearest to hand.

> POLICEMAN
> Here. In here. Everybody in here.

He herds the CHILDREN into the lavatory and slams the door behind them.

The CHILDREN stand in the centre of the lavatory, very frightened. The lavatory has been totally vandalised. It is unusable. The noise of the riot outside.

FIGG and TWENTYMAN are sitting in the waiting area.

> FIGG
> You're a teacher – you're part of it . . . why do you hang in there?

> TWENTYMAN
> In my class the children learn because they want to learn. I follow them. It's an open classroom.

> FIGG
> In a closed system.

> TWENTYMAN
> That's my way of changing things.

> FIGG
> A piss in the ocean.

> TWENTYMAN
> It makes a difference.

> FIGG
> Not with Griff sitting on your face it doesn't. Bugger your open classroom, he'll soon change all that.

> TWENTYMAN
> We'll see.

> FIGG
> They're leaning on you, brother, what are you going to do?

> TWENTYMAN
> I'm a family man with a mortgage and commitments, what do you think I'm going to do?

95   Int./Ext. School. Day.   95

At the side of the school.

BOYS and GIRLS are climbing out of the windows and running towards the action.

Sirens in the distance.

96   Ext. Playground. Day.   96

The numbers have been increased by the PUPILS who have escaped from the school, they are joining in the attack on the school. TEACHERS and POLICE are under attack from all quarters. Missiles are being found from all the usual sources: walls, tarmac, empty milk bottles in crates, etc. Fires are started.

Sirens as Police vans arrive somewhere out on the road.

97   Ext. Car park. Day.   97

Elizabeth Martlett's Mini is turned upside down.

A full scale riot is under way.

98   Int./Ext. School. Day.   98

Hysteria inside the school.

YOUNG CHILDREN are trapped inside classrooms.

TEACHERS are torn between trying to protect and quieten the frightened CHILDREN and catching those who are trying to escape.

Screams and crying from inside the classrooms.

BARRATT chases TWO OLDER BOYS down a corridor as they try to escape. The BOYS turn a firehose on BARRATT who turns and retreats.

Elizabeth Martlett's Mini goes up in a black pall of smoke and flames.

More sirens and the smashing of glass. Over this the VOICES of FIGG and TWENTYMAN are heard.

>   FIGG
> They'll make you smash up your classroom.

>   TWENTYMAN
> The kids will put it back together. You do what you can, you stay inside the system. You don't walk out on the kids.

>   FIGG
> How many teachers say that up and down the country, eh?

>   FIGG
> Labouring against the odds. Knackered at forty, screaming at the little buggers to stay in line.

>   TWENTYMAN
> Stay with it, Geoff. Lick the arses of the Board of Governors. What does it matter?

>   FIGG
>   (thinks about it)
> The state of my breath after I've been round that lot. No. Keep it, brother. Keep it.

FIGG gets up and walks off down the corridor, then returns.

>   FIGG
> Enjoy your son.

Twentyman's classroom: empty, peaceful, untouched by the riot.

The noise of the riot in the background. We glimpse some of the action out of the window.

The CAT is eating the rabbit.

Move along the images on the wall, past Nilsson's pictures, stopping at a school photograph.

It is a picture of Twentyman at school. A grammar school photograph. All the boys neatly dressed in their blazers, sitting and standing in ordered rows with their arms folded.

Next to this picture is a picture taken inside Twentyman's class. A pile of people, arms round each other, smiling, laughing, fooling around. Twentyman is in the centre of the group – a very happy man.

Published by the Press Syndicate of the University of Cambridge
The Pitt Building, Trumpington Street, Cambridge CB2 1RP
32 East 57th Street, New York, NY 10022, USA
10 Stamford Road, Oakleigh, Melbourne 3166, Australia

© Cambridge University Press 1986

First published 1986

Printed in Great Britain at the University Press, Cambridge

ISBN 0 521 31374 0

DS

A videocassette of this film is available to schools and colleges through the following British suppliers. (Please check for prices at the time of ordering.)

Concord Films Council Ltd   The Guild Organisation Ltd
201 Felixstowe Road   Guild House
Ipswich, Suffolk IP3 9BJ   Peterborough PE2 9PZ
(Videocassettes are also available for hire.)